LOCAL THEOLOGY

LOCAL THEOLOGY
Church and Community in Dialogue

JOHN READER

First published in Great Britain 1994
The Society for Promoting Christian Knowledge
Holy Trinity Church
Marylebone Road
London NW1 4DU

British Library Cataloguing-in-Publication Data
A catalogue record for this book is available from the
British Library

ISBN 0-281-04742-1

Typeset by Pioneer Associates Ltd. Perthshire
Printed in Great Britain by
Mackays of Chatham plc. Chatham Kent

Contents

Acknowledgements

First, this book is dedicated to the people of the Lydbury North Group of Parishes in Shropshire. I would also like to acknowledge the roles played by various key people outside the parishes: Richard Lewis, now Bishop of Taunton but, at the time, Archdeacon of Ludlow, and Maggie Pickup, director of the Saltley Trust, who funded and supported the local theology project throughout; Sue Johnson and Jonathan Mycock, the officers of the county organizations involved; and colleagues in the Clun Forest Deanery and at the community college in Bishops Castle: Ian Ball, Richard Beaumond, Lindsay Brown and John Reese. From the academic institutions, I am grateful for help and advice from the following: Anthony Dyson at Manchester, John Elford, now at Liverpool, Robert Morgan at Oxford, and Robin Grove-White and Brian Wynne at Lancaster. Particular thanks are due to Philip Law at SPCK, who has nursed the book through to publication. However, four friends and colleagues have probably had to endure the most debate and testing of ideas over the last few years: Ray Plant, now Lord Highfield and Master of St Catherine's College, Oxford, Andrew Buckley, Margaret Goodall, and John Atherton at Manchester. None of these people can be held responsible for what I may have failed to do in this book. Finally, thanks are due to my wife Christine, and to Kate, Simon and Thomas, for being very patient with me.

John Reader

Introduction: The Local as the Context for Theology

The importance of the local

The aim of this book is to show that it is possible for Christians who are firmly embedded in the concerns and needs of their parish and locality to engage in what I am going to call 'local theology'. At a time when far greater emphasis is being placed on the role of the laity in the ministry of the church, it is surely vital that we begin to investigate how doing theology might become a shared local activity.

I realize that in saying this I am crossing what is a well-established boundary in church life, in that theology is often seen as the preserve of the experts who have spent time and energy researching into and promulgating the sources of the Christian faith and this work then becomes a resource for those whose task it is to translate it into practical action at a local level. Parallels can be found in other professions, such as medicine and law, where there is a clear division between lay and professional and the former are always in danger of being turned into passive consumers.

However, it is open to question whether the responsibilities of living out a Christian calling and ministry benefit from being split in this fashion. On the one hand it devalues the skills and experiences of ordinary Christians and, on the other, it distances the experts from everyday practical concerns. A gap is opened up between knowledge and practice that is damaging to both aspects of ministry. Awareness of this danger is nothing new. It was Aristotle, writing from within a very different culture, who coined the term 'phronesis'—a practical wisdom that recognized the interdependence of knowledge and practice.[1] Local theology requires a similar approach, combining reference to the symbols and stories of the faith community with insights into the contemporary context that arise from non-theological sources. For many congregations, response to the immediate and local will be the focus for this process.

There is a further dimension to this discussion. Attempts to construct a local theology need to be interpreted in the wider setting of a society in which there is a growing suspicion of any group that would impose their views on others and in which individuals generally wish to exercise the right to determine beliefs and practices for themselves. Thus, concern for the local is part of a reaction against the power that is now wielded by centralized authorities in our culture. This is not to deny that these authorities have their share of people of good will, but, rather, to recognize the limitations of proposing global solutions that fail to take account of local circumstances.

The emergence of contextual theologies in other parts of the world raise a question about the unity and coherence of the Christian faith community that any local theology must address. If context is to be the determining factor in Christian thought and practice, then there is a possibility of the fragmentation of belief. We appear to be presented with two extreme alternatives: either the Christian tradition provides universal doctrines and guidelines for behaviour that then have to be applied and interpreted in every individual situation, or it is, essentially, a localized response to particular circumstances developed by those on the spot. The danger of the first option is of having nothing to say to specific groups because of the limited perspectives of the experts on which it depends. The danger of the second is of having nothing to say to the wider faith community because of the localized and idiosyncratic nature of the response. Any local theology, therefore, must steer a course between these two extremes. Engaging with the local as the initial focus for Christian ministry, then, must entail a commitment to work outwards by having an awareness of the wider picture and analysing from this broader perspective.

As the American theologian David Tracy has pointed out, starting local is an appropriate response to the fragmentation now so characteristic of the world at large:

> The groping, tentative, often conflictual and interruptive character of any of our individual interpretations of tradition and situations . . . is not a weakness but a strength. It is, more exactly, the only strength available to us: the need to interpret the plural and ambiguous tradition for an ever changing pluralistic and ambiguous situation, the need to give up the quest for an illusory ahistorical certainty and live the quest for a situated understanding of the Christian tradition in a particular place at a particular time.[2]

The local theology described in this book is part of this quest for a 'situated understanding' of the Christian tradition.

The encounter with others in a local ministry

The major argument of this book is that the search for a situated understanding of the Christian faith will involve a series of encounters with groups of people who are not regular churchgoers. The task of a local theology, therefore, is to identify ways of relating the symbols and insights of the faith community to the experiences and ideas of these other groups. As well as practical engagement, this process involves a deepening self-awareness for each of these groups, including those standing more firmly within the traditional Christian framework.

I will begin with a brief description of how I encountered

two particular groups: those on the margins of local society and those I shall describe as 'the cultured despisers of religion'.[3] I will also include the local faith community to give a complete picture. These groups arose from within a particular context, but my argument is that local theology can work out ways of relating that are based both on the specific and wider contexts.

Encountering those on the margins

One of the disappointing features of much contemporary ministry as exercised by the clergy is that it becomes focused on those who are within the fold of the local church. There are very understandable practical reasons for this. Sometimes the scale of a congregation generates demands that are all-consuming. Financial constraints are increasingly a factor for many churches and much time and energy goes into just surviving. This, unfortunately, ignores the fact that the laity are already members of other groups within the wider community and are inevitably faced with the question of how to relate their faith to these other aspects of their lives.

In smaller, rural communities, such as the one in which I was based in south-west Shropshire, however, it is often easier for a minister to encounter others outside the church. Visiting was an obvious avenue, but it was probably funerals that gave me the most crucial contacts. In this particular locality it is traditional for local people, whether churchgoers or not, to attend such services. As it became clear to them that I was happy to spend time listening to the people who did not normally come to church, people would talk to me, and, from all the different accounts, a picture of what was going on locally began to emerge.

I soon realized that the interpretations of local life I received from my immediate church contacts were founded on a narrow perspective. The established wisdom received from the regular churchgoers about the area was, in fact, the view only of the relatively affluent as theirs were the stories that had dominated the picture previously. However, as I encountered a broader cross-section of the local population, I began to be made more aware of some of the social and economic problems facing those at the lower end of the local social scale. Among these were the lack of housing, both for young people wishing to leave home and start their own families, and for workers approaching retirement who would have to vacate tied accommodation. A recent surge in house prices was one factor, but these people relied more on the rented sector—this at a time when government policy has been to sell off council property and prevent local authorities building any new social housing.

Although housing was to become a major issue, there were other related concerns for local people, in particular the threats to a whole range of facilities. The two village schools lived with the constant fear of falling numbers and consequent closure (one of them has, in fact, since been closed). The main local shop and post office survived uneasily, heavily dependent on two businesses in the village. The cottage hospital in the nearby small market town is always in danger of being closed and has had its number of beds steadily reduced. Public transport is almost non-existent. The people most dependent on these local public services are invariably the genuinely local people, most notably the elderly and young families.

What is likely to happen in these and in other similar communities is that, before long, only the affluent and the retired newcomers who have bought into the area will be able to survive there. With the decline in agriculture as an employer, the lack of alternative work and the gradual destruction of local schools, shops, hospitals and bus services, the area becomes unviable for all but a limited section of the populace. The local church might survive if it continues to court this limited section, but this would represent a failure to minister within the wider community.

Assuming that some rural areas will succeed in sustaining a balanced population, one of the challenges for local ministry will be to establish greater pastoral contact with those on the margins of both the churches and the power structures.

The cultured despisers of religion

It was through my increasing involvement with local social and political issues that I began to meet people who did not share my religious views, but who were concerned about the rapid changes affecting the locality. I discovered allies within both the Community Council of Shropshire and the Shropshire Wildlife Trust, as well as encountering others who expressed anxiety over the potential breakdown of community life and our treatment of the environment.

A particularly good example was the working relationship that developed with the Rural Officer of the Community Council. We met initially because my parishes had applied for a grant towards the cost of producing an information leaflet that we felt would be an aid to communication within the parishes and provide a reason for lay people to visit newcomers to the area.

The Rural Officer was, if anything, anti-church because of its attitude towards women. She was surprised to find herself working alongside committed Christians and discover that we are not all as dogmatic or conservative as she had expected. The work of the Community Council and local churches was clearly complementary in some instances. They had access to resources, information and skills, we had the local knowledge and contacts. Together it was possible to co-operate in locally based schemes that stood a chance of combatting the withdrawal of resources and facilities so damaging to the future of the area.

The key to this process proved to be one of the vital aspects of our local theology. How are Christians to relate to those who do not share our belief system and yet have values that motivate them towards the same practical goals? Through the projects we initiated—a local conference, examining the issues of housing, transport and community action; a play scheme, set up by local people; an environmental area on some church land; and an open group, which I shall refer to as the Local History Group—and the discussions that followed, it was possible to identify common ground and acknowledge and learn to respect genuine differences. The task was not that of conversion, but of open and respectful conversation.

It was, in fact, the Local History Group that became the major forum for such conversation. Following the model provided by the high school in the neighbouring market town, which was establishing itself as a community college, offering resources and encouragement to local groups for a variety of purposes, we gathered together people from the parishes who had expressed interest in a range of activities. Among these were the intention of taping and writing down the stories of older local people, constructing a parish map with field names and notable sites marked on it, researching the role of women in the locality in earlier centuries, and creating a local environmental project. This was a disparate group and the aim of meeting was for mutual support, information sharing, and discussion, and to enable us to invite outside speakers as appropriate.

Although church members were involved, this was not a church organization. We met first in January 1988 and then roughly every two months for the next three years. It became the powerhouse or think tank for much local action and offered a new model for church and community involvement that will be expanded on later. It was both the forum for discussions with the cultured despisers of religion and a major setting for Christians to engage in that wider reflection so essential for local theology.

The needs of the local faith community

Changes are now well under way in the rural church, and this creates both new challenges and opportunities for local congregations. Part of the story is to outline the needs generated by this process. The most obvious one is a redefinition of the roles of laity and clergy, encouraged by the reduction in numbers of full-time stipendiary clergy. Hand in hand with this goes a requirement for the laity to become more informed about their faith and, thus, more confident about practising a local ministry. A more radical question that has yet to be fully acknowledged is what type of theology is appropriate for local groups that are starting to take on greater pastoral and liturgical responsibilities? It may be that some form of local theology, as developed in this book, may have more to offer than the poor person's version of academic theology that is characteristic of many lay training courses.

Our local attempts to respond to this challenge began with a joint Parochial Church Council (PCC) meeting for my three parishes. With over seventy people present, we split up into smaller groups and identified the tasks of ministry within our area. Once these had been agreed on, we had a further discussion on the role of the full-time minister within this wider picture. Six major areas were identified: pastoral care, worship, schools and youth work, spirituality and mission, communications, and finance and administration. Working groups were formed, each with a lay convenor, that met over the next six months and then returned to another joint PCC meeting to establish a programme for future development.

Two major issues emerged from this process. First, it was clear that many church people were already exercising some form of ministry, often through informal pastoral care or related church activity. So, the objective was not to create something that did not yet exist, but, rather, to resource and support what was already happening. Second, possibly the greatest need was for people to have the opportunity to talk more openly about their beliefs *and* their doubts. Being able to do this could lead to the increased confidence so vital for effective ministry.

It was the area of pastoral care that highlighted these needs. One of the aims of the Pastoral Care Group became to meet together on an occasional basis, both for mutual support and to discuss particular concerns. We made contact with a person from a neighbouring parish who was interested in the work of Elisabeth Kübler-Ross, well known for her insights into dying and bereavement, and began to use her videos as a vehicle for further discussion.

One of the most important things that emerged from these meetings was the fact that a number of people had had experiences that did not readily fit into what might be termed 'normal' categories. Among these were near-death experiences and encounters with loved ones or other relatives after death. Most clergy will be familiar with these from post-bereavement visiting. What one makes of these descriptions is not the issue in this instance. The point is that people do not feel safe enough to talk about these experiences in a group setting. Yet, surely one of the functions of the church is to enable and encourage people to talk more freely about the spiritual dimension of their existence, whatever this may be.

The conclusion to be drawn from this is that a major contemporary challenge to local churches is to find ways of opening up discussion of the various levels of human experience in a non-judgemental and non-threatening manner. The spirituality market-place, as we might describe it, is now a growth area. This development could be interpreted as being a reaction against an overly rational and science-dominated culture that finds it difficult to acknowledge experiences which cannot be measured or verified, but the fact remains that here is an area of need to which the church is not yet responding adequately. So far, the area has been colonized either by evangelical Christians who wish to contain the experiences within strict limits, or New Age thinkers and practitioners who reject any rational dimension to spirituality. The need of the local faith community was to begin to develop an appropriate form of contemporary spirituality, one that could balance the requirements of experience, tradition and reason.

Local theology as a poppy seed head

Now that we have begun to see the challenges thrown up by analysing ministry in a particular setting, we need to discover what a local theology must look like in order to relate the symbols of the faith community to the experiences of the two other groups.

Most recent attempts to describe an experientially based approach to theology utilize the image of a circle or a spiral.[4] The great value of such images is that they emphasize that you are engaged in a dynamic thought process. Thus, you may begin by being involved in a practical issue, move on to participate in a deeper analysis of this (by using insights from the social sciences, for instance), then draw on the resources of your faith—all the time continuing to carry out an active response. In this way, theory and practice are held together. Interestingly, such a description is familiar to those involved in both adult education and community work.

Although these are helpful images, they do tend to impose the idea of unified and coherent development on the whole process, which rarely happens in real life. This, though, is just one way of looking at what happens, and there are others. I would prefer to describe the process in less conclusive terms as, in my experience, direct practical involvement can lead out in a whole variety of directions and draw on resources, both theological and non-theological, that never do actually lead back to the starting point.

A more appropriate picture, in the light of this, is the poppy seed head. The encounter with a particular problem is the stimulus for action, which can be likened to the breeze that blows the seed head. The effect of this is that the poppy seeds are blown out in many different directions; there is an explosion of energy. Not all of the seeds will germinate, but no one can know in advance what will come of this release of potential: some of the growth may happen at a distance from the original poppy; some of it may be of obvious benefit to the original site; it may well not be possible to hold the developments together in a coherent picture or to make sense of them as a whole. The subsequent process, therefore, is altogether more random and fragmented than the image of the spiral implies; it cannot be restricted to or contained in such a neat formula.

Reason and the local

If we are to build on the image of the poppy seed head, we are faced with a serious question about the role of human reason in the process of local theology. If the picture is so confused, how might it be possible for human beings to construct any order and meaning out of this chaos?

On one level, reason is, after all, a human attempt to provide frameworks and patterns in life so that we may move with some coherence and confidence from one situation to another. What I want to do now, however, is fine tune this idea a bit and suggest that concern for the local, as an appropriate starting point for doing theology, stands firmly within a growing tradition which holds that reason works from inside particular contexts rather than being an over-arching method transcending all possible contexts. In other words, we are not talking about a universal concept of reason that applies in all times and in all places, but, rather, about the ways of working that develop on the ground as people attempt to work things out as they go along. This, too, is *human* reason—neither so universal as to be set at an impossible distance from real, human affairs, nor so particular that it cannot be identified in radically different settings and still provide a framework for human action and communication.

11

A description of the issue from within moral philosophy may help to illuminate it for us. Michael Walzer in his book on justice suggests that there are two ways of approaching the subject.[5] The first, perhaps original, way:

> . . . is to walk out of the cave, leave the city, climb the mountain, fashion for oneself (what never can be fashioned for ordinary men and women) an objective and universal standpoint. Then one describes the terrain of everyday life from far away, so that it loses its particular contours and takes on a general shape.[6]

What Walzer is proposing, by contrast, is to stand *in* the cave, *in* the city, and *on* the ground. The task then becomes that of interpreting the world of meanings, which is already shared, to our fellow citizens. It is impossible to create a just society from scratch, but we can try to work out together what *might* be required given current attitudes and circumstances. Local theology will be like this to the extent that it starts in the cave and on the ground, but it will have to be *more* than this, given the need to converse with those from other caves. If there is to be *real* communication, we must be prepared to move away from the safe ground and put some of our beliefs to the test. What do we have to help us as we move out of the cave and into unfamiliar territory?

Mediating frameworks for a local theology

In the remainder of this introduction, I am going to offer three provisional mediating frameworks that may assist on the journey. It is important to clarify the status of these. They are not another set of universal concepts or structures for which I am claiming an objective validity. Neither are they meant to be so localized as to be of no practical use beyond the context in which they have been developed. They may be of value on some occasions but not all, and they must always remain open to revision and re-description. However, they will serve as a starting point for the time being. What I will argue is that the three frameworks are responses to the three areas of concern already identified in the first part of this introduction.

As the concept of a mediating framework is so central to the argument for a local theology, I will expand on it briefly. First, it must be distinguished from the notion of middle axioms—an idea put forward by William Temple earlier this century to relate Christian doctrine to specific political and social issues. The crucial difference is that Temple was trying to argue down from universal moral principles to the particular situation. In contrast, mediating frameworks are designed to move in exactly the *opposite* direction. Theology in this form *begins* with the local engagement and *then* utilizes the frameworks to discover wider and more general applications.

The second point is to link the concept with the work of Jürgen Habermas—a contemporary German philosopher and sociologist who is searching for an approach to ethics that does not admit the universal claims of any one tradition, but discovers common ground in the human practices of argumentation.[7] This is not the place to enter into a detailed discussion of his ideas, but it is worth mentioning six aspects of his integrating frameworks in order to highlight parallels and differences. For Habermas, such frameworks must be nonfoundationalist, interdisciplinary, search for a coherence of different perspectives, concentrate on forms rather than content, oppose relativism, and isolate structures or stages in the process in question as the unifying factors. Although this seems complicated, the basic thrust of the concept is very similar to that of a mediating framework. The major difference, which will become clear shortly, is that I believe there must be room in any framework for the content of particular traditions. Only on the basis of a commitment to respect and honour other people will there be a willingness to enter into the open discussions such frameworks demand.

What we now require are mediating frameworks that will facilitate the making of links between the two groups identified from the Shropshire story and those within the faith community. These connections cannot be made solely on the basis of local experience, but must employ reflection and analysis on a wider spectrum of concerns. In order to assist in the process, we will draw on resources that are appropriate for the particular group.

Relating to those on the margins

The main source for this framework is liberation theology. There are obvious reasons for this. First, as with many other contextual theologies, liberation theology takes as its starting point the experiences of those on the margins of society. Second, it attempts to establish a prophetic perspective on current social and political injustices with a view to working towards a more just society. Third, it takes seriously the issue of power, which is an inescapable dimension in any form of social analysis that is to speak to the needs of the marginalized. Finally, it is not afraid to employ methods of social analysis that do not derive from Christian sources. These four elements offer us clues as to the nature of a local theology relevant to this group.

A local theology will take as its starting point the stories and accounts of those who are most deeply and seriously affected by contemporary social changes. This means listening to the voices of those least able—for personal and economic reasons—to cope with the forces in our culture that may well benefit a majority of people, but only at the cost of the deprivation of others. Among these forces we might identify, particularly, the growing individualism of our culture—the predominance of self-interest as a motivating political factor, concern for short-term profitability at the expense of social need, and a limiting view of what it is to be a human being, which reduces individuals and communities to means serving economic ends.

Introduction: The Local Context

Unless the voices of those who are at the sharp end of these social and political trends can be listened to, there is no chance of developing a theology that not only makes contact with, but takes as a touchstone of our culture those who are on the margins of society. Engaging in the process of local theology in this way I would see as both a moral and pastoral necessity.

The second element in the process will then be to draw on the critical analyses of contemporary life, offered in particular by the social sciences. In other words, it will not do simply to offer a sympathetic ear to those in need. We must work together to understand the economic and political forces that create or sustain these needs. This is no easy task, particularly as few church people, let alone theologians, have the necessary skills and knowledge in the fields of social and political analysis. However, the task is an essential one if we are not to be drawn into action and reaction in a naive and uncritical manner. It may be that not everybody will be able to contribute to this level of the process, but then it places a considerable responsibility for clear presentation and communication on to those who do have the time and energy to give to the work of analysis. One of the major failings of many well-meaning church reports and statements on contemporary issues is their unwillingness to enter into the debates in sufficient depth.[3]

Any local theology must also, of course, make reference to the familiar sources of our own tradition—Scripture, its subsequent interpretations by fellow Christians—and, indeed, the experiences of Christians in other places struggling with similar problems. We do this not in order to read answers to current problems straight out of these sources, but in order to maintain the discussion with fellow Christians through common language and symbols. What constitutes an appropriate use of Christian sources may become clearer as we investigate further the development of a contemporary spirituality.

Finally, local theology must be based on, and feed back

15

into, local, practical engagement with the issues at hand. All the reflection in the world will be of no earthly use unless it both sustains and provides critical perspectives on the work that we do. Here we see that localized version of human reason in action—thinking things out as we go along, being prepared to revise and rethink as well as to react, offering frameworks that may be of use to others in similar situations. Works and faith should go hand in hand.

In summary then, the ideas emerging from liberation theology that inform a local theology lead to this four-fold structure: listening to the local stories, drawing on contemporary analytical frameworks such as sociology and psychology, drawing on Christian sources, and then direct engagement with local issues and needs. This is our first mediating framework.

Relating to the cultured despisers

How are Christians to enter into discussion with the cultured despisers of religion, those who do not share their assumptions and beliefs and yet who face up to and try to articulate the questions that confront all of us at this late stage in the twentieth century? In order to answer this question, I suggest a brief examination of the intellectual environment that is now described by some as modernity–post-modernity.[9]

Perhaps the most significant aspect of this environment, from our point of view, is that this is the era of the breakdown of all 'grand narratives'. A grand narrative is a picture or world view that claims to offer a total explanation of both our individual and communal lives. Thus, most major religions, including Christianity, are grand narratives, as, indeed, is Marxism, and the hope in human reason represented by the Enlightenment. What has happened over the last 200 years is that each of these master stories has been challenged and undermined by further intellectual exploration. According to the post-modern view, it is no longer possible to claim that any one narrative can offer a definitive, universal, exhaustive, true-for-all-time description of the way things are. What we have is a situation in which there are a number of competing, often conflicting, major narratives that offer partial and fragmented accounts of human existence.

It is the awareness of the uncertainty and insecurity created by this intellectual climate that lies at the heart of much contemporary thought, and, indeed, of many of the more radical social movements.[10] Christianity is faced with two options, it seems to me: either to deny these current feelings and insights into the human condition and to go on staking its claims to offer a universal explanation of reality, or to accept its place in this confusion and acknowledge that it is only one of a number of major narratives offering partial insights and interpretations. If we are to engage with those who are at the sharp end of contemporary thinking, then, I believe, we must be prepared to take the second option and accept the limited nature of the Christian narrative.

Some will find such a suggestion horrifying and, indeed, threatening, but I would recommend that they begin to look closely at their own beliefs and patterns of living in order to see just how much or how little they actually derive from identifiable Christian sources. I suspect that most of us belong to and move around within a number of major narratives. Those who claim that they belong exclusively to one narrative are fundamentalists. Those who still wish to hold on to one major narrative as being *the* key to all the rest, that by which all others are to be judged, are in a slightly less dogmatic position, but will need to face the challenge nevertheless.

There is a great fear of what is often described as relativism, as if this automatically meant that one had to abandon any claims for the insights of one's own tradition. This does not follow, nor is it possible, in practical terms, to live this way. We *have* to make assumptions about what we believe to be trustworthy and true in order to carry out the most basic of daily tasks, and we do, in fact, use as a basis ideas about the wider reality in order to function in our relationships with others. We conduct our lives 'as if' certain things were true, and that, it seems to me, is wholly necessary and perfectly legitimate. It is, though, our willingness to acknowledge the provisional and fragmented nature of our understanding of the world that is the key to our relationships with those who do not share our Christian major narrative.

I want to suggest, then, that the tasks of a post-modern Christianity will be something like this. First, we need to become more aware of the major narratives that are at work inside ourselves. Second, we need to be willing to bracket or to let go of those major narratives enough to be able to listen to others who live with different narratives. Third, one of the most valuable services that the church has to offer is the opportunity to create spaces within which others can share their stories and listen and learn without entering into direct conflict. We must accept our differences without abandoning our own beliefs. Finally, we must recognize and identify the elements within our own tradition that both facilitate and encourage this process of sharing. For instance, I would want to say that the language of parts of the Christian mystical tradition that describes the experience of letting go, of leaving behind familiar structures of thought and behaviour in order to become part of a greater reality, is of particular value here.[11] This is, already, an approach to spirituality that links with a post-modern understanding.

The structure of a contemporary spirituality

The main reason for including among our resources for ministry the areas of faith development and spirituality is in order to acknowledge the various dimensions of human nature that contribute to our religious responses. We have seen that a major need of those within the faith community is to acknowledge that theology is more than an intellectual exercise. What I want to do now is to present a further mediating framework that may help us to move beyond the local to a greater degree of generality. As before, I am not claiming a universal, objective validity for what follows, merely suggesting that it may help us to interpret some of what is going on some of the time.

Although the stages of faith development that are particularly associated with the work of James Fowler have been an influence on this framework, it does differ from them in significant respects.[12] It also draws on the ideas of an American sociologist of religion, Ken Wilbur[13] and the British sociologist Anthony Giddens.[14]

Where I differ from Fowler is in the notion that it is possible to identify a process of development in the journey of faith. According to Fowler, we each move through a series of stages or different ways of understanding our religious beliefs as we progress through life. There are inherent dangers in such an approach, however, that I wish to avoid. First, Fowler claims an empirical basis for his work, in the form of research that has been conducted. The problem with this is that the sections of the population researched have been so limited as to leave the theory open to the charge of only applying to a narrow category of people—invariably white, well-educated, middle-class males. Indeed, significant critiques of the model have been launched from a feminist perspective, so it is not clear that it can readily be used in contexts other than those researched.[15] I want to make no such objective claims for what I am going to propose; it is just another picture or story that might illuminate some aspects of our lives.

Second, the very idea of development is culturally loaded, as has been pointed out by John Hull.[16] It suggests that movement in a particular direction is a good thing and that failure to move in that way should be an automatic cause for concern. What begins as being descriptive ends up becoming normative. This may not have been Fowler's intention, but it is hard to escape this implication of his work. It also means

19

that his stages can be used as a way of exercising power over others by saying that a person should have reached a specific stage by now. What I propose does not represent a chronological development, but, rather, a way of understanding the different levels at which we operate throughout our lives. In other words, we move from one level to another at any time, regardless of age.

I believe it is useful to say that there are four basic levels at which human beings function. The first we may call the unconscious. Without going into detailed argument, I would describe this as the parts of ourselves of which we are not normally aware, but that, nevertheless, affect the ways in which we think, feel, and behave. That there *is* such a level we know from, initially, Freud,[17] but his ideas have been taken further and are now central to the discipline of psychology. It may be that it is useful to suggest that there are different levels within the unconscious itself, but that degree of elaboration seems unnecessary here.[18] The debate about the origins of these unconscious influences is equally interesting, complicated, and not for us to enter into here. I do not want to attribute objective or 'scientific' status to any of these theories in any case, but merely point out that they are one way we have at the moment of talking about ourselves, and, in particular, the possible influences on our behaviour of which we are not fully aware.

The second level is described by Giddens as 'practical consciousness'.[19] This is a way of describing how most of us are most of the time in our waking lives. It means that we are engaged in the normal routine of daily life in a fairly unreflective and mechanical way, just getting on with familiar tasks in a familiar environment. When people talk about having a 'simple faith', I think it is this level of operation they are describing. I do not mean this in a derogatory way, simply that this is the way we do have to be much of the time simply in order to live. That is, we learn how to do things and appropriate ways of behaving in particular circumstances so that we do not have to spend time and energy thinking things out and making new decisions on every single occasion. Other ways of describing this might be as living within a tradition,[20] a lifeworld,[21] or plausability structure,[22] or as obeying custom or acting out of habit. I would suggest that many regular churchgoers operate on this level—and, possibly, the first level as well—in most of their religious activities. We may also want to describe this as an experiential dimension of faith, although I would not want to rule out the possibility of this being applicable at another level.

The third level I want to term 'critical consciousness'. By this I mean the times when, either as a matter of choice or necessity, we stand back from everyday operations and beliefs and begin to review them in a more critical and questioning manner. In our personal lives, this might mean attempting to identify the unconscious influences on our behaviour. In contemporary culture, this is often done through counselling or therapy.[23] In social and political relationships, it may mean entering into debates about justice or equality and attempting to understand the nature of moral argument.[24] In the framework for local theology, this level clearly corresponds to a critical, often academic approach to our faith under the impact of alternative patterns of belief.

In a pluralistic culture, where we can no longer take our tradition or lifeworld for granted, we are forced to first question and then defend to others the positions and beliefs we hold.[25] Much of what is going on currently in both clergy and lay training is attempting to shift people's modes of operating to the third level by means of a process of consciousness-raising and creating greater self-awareness. I suspect that much local and contextual theology is also working at this level and that this parallels other social movements in contemporary society.[26]

The fourth level is much more difficult to pin down. I will describe it as 'transrational' or 'transpersonal consciousness'. It is important to include it in the overall framework because it represents a genuine human aspiration. Fowler's sixth stage may be related to this,[27] although I have found Wilbur's seventh, eighth and ninth stages, which are based on so-called mystical experience and the theories of psychosynthesis, more helpful.[28] This allows for what have been called 'altered states of consciousness',[29] within which people appear to lose sight of the normal boundaries between themselves and the rest of the world. Thus, they report a sense of being at one with both other people and the whole of creation, of no longer feeling themselves to be isolated individuals.

The danger with this level is that it could actually be a regression to the first level. One of the tasks suggested by Wilbur is to find criteria for discriminating between the first and fourth levels. One of the problems with the contemporary search for an ecological spirituality is that it might merely represent just such a regression.[30] It is the link between environmental concerns and spirituality that will be the focus in Chapter 6.

What I want to suggest is that we refrain from describing any experience as being at the fourth level unless it can be shown that it has passed through the third level. A spirituality that bypasses awareness of and involvement in social and political issues is not really engaging the full human being and is, thus, incomplete. The process of detachment normally associated with spirituality needs to be clearly linked to the activity associated with social and political commitment if there is to be anything like a full picture of the range of human spirituality.

In summary, then, our third mediating framework proposing a contemporary spirituality looks like this:

- first level, the unconscious
- second level, practical consciousness
- third level, critical consciousness
- fourth level, transrational or transpersonal consciousness.

The plan of the book

The rest of the book will follow the process of doing local theology through the story of each of the three groups mentioned earlier. The first chapter will examine the key issue for those on the margins of local society, that of housing. Having heard the accounts in greater detail, we will then use the framework suggested by liberation theology to engage in wider discussion and analysis. In particular, we will focus on the issue of power, relating this to questions of church involvement in community work and where this might lead.

The third chapter returns us to the encounters with those who share our social concerns but not our specific religious commitment. The accounts here will revolve around one of the community projects and the work of the Local History Group. The discussion will then widen out in Chapter 4 to consider the questions raised by post-modernity and how Christianity might respond to this new situation, if such it is.

Chapter 5 examines the attempts of a church group to establish an environmental area on church property and the issues this brought to the surface. How we relate to the natural world has become a major focus for the development of a contemporary spirituality and I will move on in Chapter 6 to examine how the structure suggested in the third mediating framework offers criteria for assessing such developments. The seventh chapter will consider how local theology links with the approach of what are called 'new social movements' and give glimpses of the church of the future. Will increasing fragmentation and individualization destroy congregational life as we know it now, or will it lead to new, more flexible patterns of belief and practice that will maintain continuity with the faith communities of the past? Can there be a centre that will hold while all else changes and, if not, what will remain of the Christian tradition?

Notes

1 Aristotle, *Ethics* (Penguin 1974), p. 181.
2 Hans Küng and David Tracy, eds, *Paradigm Change in Theology* (T. & T. Clark 1989), essay by David Tracy.
3 Friedrich Schleiermacher, *On Religion: Speeches to Its Cultured Despisers*. New York, Harper & Row, 1958.
4 Laurie Green, *Let's Do Theology* (Mowbray 1990), p. 30. Joe Holland and Peter Henriot, *Social Analysis* (New York, Orbis, 1985), p. 8.
5 Michael Walzer, *Spheres of Justice*. Basil Blackwell 1983.
6 Walzer, p. xiv.
7 Jürgen Habermas, *Moral Consciousness and Communicative Action*. Polity Press 1990.
8 See for instance article by John Reader, 'The Church, State and Civil Society' in *Southwell & Oxford Papers on Contemporary Society* (Summer Issue 1989) on the failure of *Faith in the City* to take into account the political arguments of the New Right.
9 Richard J. Bernstein, *The New Constellation*. Polity Press 1991.
10 Margaret Goodall and John Reader, 'Environmentalism as the Question of Human Identity' in Ian Ball, Margaret Goodall, Clare Palmer and John Reader, eds, *The Earth Beneath*. SPCK 1992.
11 Robert K. C. Forman, *Meister Eckhart: Mystic as Theologian*. Element Books 1991.
12 James Fowler, *Stages of Faith*. New York, Harper & Row, 1981.
13 Ken Wilbur, *A Sociable God*. Boulder, CO , Shambhala, 1983.
14 Anthony Giddens, *The Constitution of Society*. Polity Press 1984.
15 Sharon Daloz Parks, 'The North American Critique of James Fowler's Theory of Faith Development' in James W. Fowler, Karl Ernst Nipkow, and Friedrich Schweitzer, eds, *Stages of Faith and Religious Development*. SCM Press 1992.
16 John Hull, 'Human Development and Capitalist Society' in Fowler, Nipkow, and Schweitzer.
17 Don Cupitt, *What is a Story?* (SCM Press 1991), p. 46.
18 See for instance Jean Hardy, *Psychology with a Soul*. Aquarius 1986.
19 Giddens, p. 41.
20 Hans-Georg Gadamer, *Truth and Method*. Sheed & Ward 1975.

21 Jürgen Habermas, *The Theory of Communicative Action*, Vol. 1 (Boston, Beacon Press ,1984), p. 70.

22 Peter Berger, *A Rumour of Angels*. Penguin 1970.

23 Anthony Giddens, *Modernity and Self-Identity* (Polity Press 1991), p. 71.

24 Alberto Melucci, *Nomads of the Present* (Hutchinson Radius 1989), p. 41.

25 Jürgen Habermas in Peter Dews, ed., *Habermas: Autonomy and Solidarity* (Verso 1986), p. 54.

26 John Reader, 'Local Theology and the New Social Movements' in *Modern Churchman*, New Series, Vol. XXXII, No. 4, 1991.

27 Fowler, p. 199ff.

28 Wilbur, p. 27ff.

29 Forman, p. 151ff.

30 Margaret Goodall and John Reader, 'Why Fox Fails to Change the World' in Ball, Goodall, Palmer, and Reader, op. cit.

1

Housing and Questions of Power

Rural housing

When the local theology project began in the mid 1980s, it was only just starting to be acknowledged that there was such a thing as a rural housing problem. Certain agencies, notably the National Agricultural Centre Rural Trust and Community Councils, were attempting to establish the issue on both local and national political agendas. Since then, vigorous campaigning and much publicity have raised the profile of the need for local homes for local people. However, efforts to tackle this have not done much more than scratch the surface. If anything, the problems are getting worse. With the rising interest rates and mortgage repayments of the early 1990s, the number of homeless people nationally is still increasing. Proposed solutions are not even coping with the existing level of need, let alone a deteriorating situation.

It looks as though shortage of available and suitable property at prices or rents within the range of poorer people is going to be one of the most serious social problems for some years to come. The account that follows of a local manifestation of this needs to be seen in this wider context. This is far from being a purely rural concern. One of the difficulties that we had to face when the local process began was that lack of housing was seen solely as an urban problem. The prevalent image of the countryside is still one of tranquil harmony and affluence. Part of the task was to shatter this illusion and reveal the forms of deprivation that exist.

The causes of the housing problem in rural areas are complicated. It is too simplistic to attribute it wholly to an influx of wealthy newcomers pushing up property prices, although this has undoubtedly been a factor. Government policy on the sale of council houses is another possible cause, but one must discuss, too, the values that lie behind such a policy.

The aim of this chapter is to describe how the issue became established through the work of the local theology project and to reflect on the further questions that were raised by this. In particular, it became clear that local housing offered a focus for other issues, notably those of power and local democracy. The meaning of community was another major consideration, but this will be developed in the next chapter.

Raising public awareness

Much credit is due to the publication *The People, the Land and the Church.*[1] Although the book itself contained important accounts and statistics, its more important function was to offer an opportunity for publicity for the issue and public debate. National newspapers and magazines responded to the book by taking up the story. In national terms, this contributed power to the pressure already being exerted by the organizations mentioned above. Locally however, it was even more significant, as it forced the subject to people's attention and legitimized more open discussion.

As with all such campaigns, the effects are cumulative and those most concerned have to be prepared to persist in consciousness-raising tactics until a breakthrough occurs and the issue is taken up by the politicians. Realizing this was part of the learning process for the local history group. We began with some knowledge of individual family's difficulties in finding accommodation, but with very limited understanding of the true scale of the problem, or of what might be done to tackle it. After two years of deeper involvement, we were much better informed on both counts. We had also gained considerable experience of dealing with local politicians and their officers. The process involved the acquisition of skills and confidence as well as knowledge—there was much more to it than just local housing.

Our initial encounter with the problem occurred because the Vicar and church wardens of one of the parishes were trustees of a school house. When the school itself had been built in the 1840s, the house was included as accommodation for the headmaster or headmistress. As with many village schools, no member of staff had wished to take advantage of this for some years. The Local Education Authority however had continued to utilize the property for staff working elsewhere. In April 1986, these tenants left and the Education Authority decided that they had no further need of the house and so handed it back to the trustees. They demanded that a separate entrance be made to avoid future occupants driving into the school playground, as this was the only access. Although this was a reasonable request, the trustees had no money to pay for this work to be done. The only asset they had was the house itself.

This led to a stalemate between the Education Authority and the trustees, with the former being unwilling to allow the trustees to do anything at all with the property and the trustees being financially unable to comply with the requirements for separate access. Discussions took place with the diocesan authorities to see if they would be prepared to contribute the necessary finance. However, no progress was made on that front either and, after two years, the property was still empty and starting to deteriorate as a result.

By this time, it was known locally that the house was vacant and a number of young couples came to the vicarage and asked me if they could rent the property from the trustees. All of them were in unsatisfactory, short-term lets and in need of more adequate accommodation. I had to tell them that we were not in a position to rent the house out because of this stalemate with the Education Authority. This explanation was neither appreciated nor understood and I could see why. The impression that the trustees were giving to local people was that we were playing for time, waiting for the school to close (there was a threat of this on the horizon even then) in order to sell the whole property to the highest bidder. At a time when the fact of a housing shortage was entering the public consciousness, this seemed an appalling witness for the local church to be giving. Surely, we should have been expressing our pastoral concern for local families by making this property available.

It is important to recognize both how complicated and how frustrating such issues rapidly become. From the local point of view the task was simple, to release the property into the rented sector. However, the more we examined the options, the more impossible achieving this aim appeared to be. By the time we had dealt with the Education Authority, the diocese, two housing associations, the Housing Corporation (and thus government policy), plus charity commissioners, there were so many rules and regulations standing in our way that the whole enterprise seemed out of reach. Meantime, the property remained empty and the church appeared not to be concerned with real local problems.

The breakthrough came as a result of a chance discussion with a recently appointed officer of South Shropshire District Council. The plan was to put in a bid for what is known as 'slippage money'—the amount left over at the end of each financial year in housing corporation funds that it is in their interest to spend in order to be given the same size grant for the following year. This can mean sums in the order of tens of thousands. If the District Council could negotiate on our behalf to release some of this money to the Housing Association of Wolverhampton, they could then carry out the necessary work on the school house, lease it from the trustees and so make it available to rent to a local family. This had not been done before, as far as was known, but, given that all else had failed, we had nothing to lose by trying it. At this stage we entrusted the negotiations to the officer of the District Council.

What can be learned from this is that if local people are to effectively confront these problems, which are so bound up with local and national politics, they need the help and expertise of people within the system who know and understand it. They also need to gain a working knowledge of such systems for themselves. Disparities in power are sustained or heightened because of different levels of knowledge of and access to the decision-making bodies. It is the most affluent and the most powerful who invariably possess the greater knowledge and, thus, have an immediate advantage in playing the system or working it to their own benefit. We were fortunate enough to gain the help of a sympathetic officer in a key position who could see loopholes and steer a plan through them.

Even then, the process was not straightforward and it took a further two years before the scheme came to fruition and a local family finally took up residence. It also involved detailed legal work. Luckily one of the trustees knew a solicitor, but without specialized support it would have been very difficult to see the scheme through to completion.

It should be clear from this story that this stage of the process of local theology involves direct action, finding appropriate ways to deal with issues that are of immediate concern. In another instance, this could call for engagement in a totally different activity, but there is always a strong possibility that it will entail dealing with statutory or political organizations of some kind. We learned just how little we knew about the workings of such bodies and how important it is to become better informed if we are to play a more effective role.

The second part of this local story illustrates what can be learned from attempts to make local democracy operate more effectively. Once again, it was the housing problem that was the occasion for this learning.

A local housing survey

Following a deanery conference on the concerns raised by *The People, the Land and the Church*, we issued all participants with a questionnaire that asked them what they thought was the most important local issue and for their views as to what future action should be taken. We received a good number of replies, most of which highlighted the problem of lack of housing for local young people. This was fed directly back into the church system through meetings of PCCs. The PCC in one local village discussed the problem at length, including the role played by government policy on council housing and, as a result, sent a letter to the Parish Council suggesting that it carry out a housing needs survey in order to establish the level of need.

This was a tactic recommended by the two organizations already fully involved in the debate, based on their experience of effective local action. Most parish councils consider themselves helpless in the face of major policy decisions as they have few real powers. However, setting up a needs survey is something they can do effectively, with the advice of either a community or district council. A subsidiary aim of this process, then, was to mobilize the Parish Council. Another important consideration was that the Parish Council is, in theory, the most appropriate local body to carry this out as it is democratically elected and so more representative of the range of village interests than any other organization. Beyond that, it seemed that a good needs survey could establish convincingly whether or not there was a local problem. It had already been shown that the District Council's housing waiting lists were not an accurate guide because people would not make applications for property in villages where there was no prospect of any building. This did not mean, however, that they would not want to live or remain in their own community if property were to be made available.

Unfortunately, we received a negative response from the Parish Council, but they did suggest that if the church carried out such a survey, they would be interested to hear the results. This was at the beginning of 1988. Nothing much happened for the next twelve months. Then the question was raised again at a PCC meeting and the Parish Council's lack of interest commented upon.

The PCC wrote to the Parish Council once again, urging some immediate action. This time we were informed that an invited speaker was coming to the Parish Council's Annual General Meeting to talk about rural housing. This seemed like a step in the right direction, but the speaker turned out to be the local district councillor rather than someone from the Community Council or from the National Agricultural Centre Rural Trust, either of whom could have offered a wider perspective. This meeting, the first part of which was open to the public and to which non-councillors could contribute, was clearly going to be critical.

The meeting itself was well attended. Unfortunately the picture painted for us by the speaker was a depressing one, giving the impression that there was nothing that could be done about the problem, certainly at parish level. The one thing not mentioned was the possibility of a housing needs survey. This was raised from the floor during the plenary question session. However, we were told that it would be too expensive and that the Parish Council had not got the resources to carry out such a survey. One member of the public offered to do the necessary photocopying for nothing and I was sure other people would volunteer their services free of charge, but this had no effect.

Although the discussion got more heated, it looked as though the issue, and, therefore, the possibility of any local action, would be lost. However, one member of the public, rapidly losing patience with the proceedings, suggested a show of hands from the floor to indicate the strength of public feeling regarding the survey. The councillor chairing this section of the meeting agreed and everybody not on the council put up their hands in favour. This was the turning point, because it was then clear that the Parish Council had to be seen to do something in order to placate public opinion and retain credibility. Lesson number one in local politics: if you want the politicians to take an issue on board, you first have to convince them that they will lose votes or public support if they do not.

Once the decision had been made to carry out a survey, events moved swiftly and it was completed within a few months.

The after-effects of this public confrontation lasted within the community. Comments about the church meddling in politics were made and part of the argument was that open confrontation was automatically a bad thing, particularly when it involved leading members of the community. What has to be noted, however, is that the way power had been handled in the Parish Council made confrontation the *only* means available for bringing the issue out into the open. Those who have power do not need to do anything in order to maintain their position; those who want change have to confront them and risk being dubbed troublemakers.

The survey revealed that there was a need in the parish for fifty-one housing units over the next five years. This figure came as a surprise even to those of us who had recognized that there was such a need as we had thought it might be nearer ten or twelve. There could be no doubt now that there was a genuine problem. The Parish Council was one of the first in this part of the county to conduct such a survey. It worked closely with both the District Council and the Community Council and received well-earned praise for its efforts at this level. The next stage in the process was to find some land on which a development might happen, preferably outside the existing planning envelope. Also, a housing association would need to be convinced that this was a viable project.

The experience of those already involved in housing projects was that no housing association would consider a development in a parish that was in any way divided over the question of whether or not there should be a scheme of this sort. Another encouraging aspect of the survey was that, out of the 78 per cent of returned forms (itself an unusually high figure for such a survey), only two people expressed opposition to such a scheme. This seemed to indicate a community concern for the needs of local people and the effectiveness of the consciousness-raising that had taken place over the previous two years.

The importance of the process just described must not be underestimated. Most opposition to local housing projects stems from a denial of there being a problem in the first place. In other words, the thinking is 'there are no homeless people around here'. Once people have been made to face the fact that there *are* homeless local people, they are much more likely to feel obliged to respond—certainly in rural areas such as this. Those of us who had been trying to establish housing as an issue, particularly within the local group, had talked about it formally and informally on so many occasions that we knew the subject inside out and were weary of having to repeat the same arguments. However, it was essential that we kept repeating them until the breakthrough finally came. Lesson number two in local politics: keep going no matter how long it takes—you will get there in the end, with a bit of luck.

Wider issues

As mentioned earlier consciousness-raising and all that it involves is important. This applies in many different contexts. There is also a need to find your way around relevant organizations, political or otherwise, and to recruit key people sympathetic to your aims who know how to play the system. The nature of power is an issue that recurs inescapably. So often, well-meaning groups become involved in local concerns without knowing what they are letting themselves in for and are forced to retreat as a result of lack of skill and information. Knowing how power works leads to attempts to correct imbalances and efforts being made that stand some chance of success. Making local democracy more effective is a vital task in so many instances. Democratic structures are invariably neutralized by older or more powerful networks that operate things to their own advantage.

Behind all this lie questions of value. Why should it be important to provide local homes for local people at all? In a society where people are encouraged to exercise individual choice above everything else, why should there be provision for those who cannot afford to purchase their own property in an area? Surely they can choose to move somewhere else? This view only makes sense, though, if you are one of the more affluent members of society, able to exercise the right to choose. Those with less money have less choice. This is what has already happened in many rural parishes where only the retired and affluent can afford the property and the locals have long since moved into the cities. Does this matter though?

As a point of Christian principle, the local history group felt that it could not accept current social policies unquestioningly. There was talk of the need for balanced communities where there were still *local* people and, indeed, *young* people. Beneath this lies a vision of community that will be developed in Chapter 2—that there should be room for variety and difference and a guarding against exclusive groupings. There was also a concern for those who are always the first victims of social change (those most vulnerable to changes in agriculture in this context). This conflicts with the priority afforded to choice in current policies and must also challenge the principle of home ownership so deeply embedded in the notion of popular capitalism.

One final point. Part of the problem of putting so much

35

time and energy into the local housing debate was that other concerns received too little attention. We reached a stage where we felt we had made ground in this area only to discover that we faced threats to other local services, such as school transport and cottage hospitals. It needs to be noted that single-issue campaigns, while good for focusing support and ideas, can sometimes divert attention away from other areas of concern. The only way round this that we thought of was the possibility of setting up an organization with representatives from all local bodies, particularly those most at risk, whose task it would be to monitor and respond in detail to any proposed policy changes that would affect the area. They could produce 'community impact statements', for want of a better phrase. It was pointed out that parish councils are supposed to fulfil this function. However, this does not answer the question who does this if the parish council will not? The local church may have a role to play here, but only as instigator, not as representative of all local interests. If democracy is to work, it needs to be rethought at this level of operation.

Questions of power

Questions about the nature of power recurred throughout the local theology project, so it seems only reasonable to suggest that this constitutes an inescapable dimension of a local theology concerned with those on the margins. One definition of power might be the capacity to shape the future in a different way. For those at the cutting edge of social change, the objective will be to ensure that everyone has a say in determining their own future. This cannot happen without exercising power.

Although there have been attempts to analyse power theologically, perhaps most notably by Paul Tillich and Reinhold Niebuhr,[2] I will here draw on sociological sources as we move on to reflect on the issues raised by our encounter with local housing problems. The main reason for this is that certain strands of sociology provide us with more appropriate tools for analysing the specific and local.

A sociology of power

There is a tendency to associate power with the operations of government and large organizations, to define it in terms familiar to the powerful within society. While this is clearly valuable, it leaves questions about normal, everyday life unanswered and can suggest that we should not *expect* to find power working at this level. However, my experiences contradict such an assumption, for it quickly became clear that power *was* being exercised within parish councils and indeed PCCs. Are there frameworks of interpretation or insights that we could borrow from sociology to illuminate the nature of power as it is experienced at micro and local levels?

The first question that arises is that of the sources of power. In this particular community, a section of it perceived itself to be almost totally powerless in the face of the influence exerted by the large landowners in the area. I want to refer to the work of Anthony Giddens in order to help us understand what was going on here.[3]

According to Giddens, power is exercised by controlling two types of resources. The first of these he calls 'allocative resources', meaning what is available within the natural world, such as raw materials and land itself. The second source is derived from influence within the social world, the authority that is present within relationships. Power is, therefore, generated and reproduced through these structures of domination. How does this analysis clarify the local experience?

The ownership of land was obviously a major source of power in that part of Shropshire. It was not simply control over the land itself that contributed to this, but the structures associated with it in a predominantly agricultural setting. Farming is still the major source of employment and also of housing for a significant proportion of the population. This creates a dependence that is deliberately fostered and sustained by the landowners as they need to retain an available and quiescent labour force. On one local estate, none of the workers were allowed to belong to a union. How such a disparity of power had been able to be enforced over centuries is difficult to understand, unless we can grasp the importance of the control exercised by the few over the allocative resources.

Giddens suggests that, with the growth of capitalism, authoritative resources become more significant. Thus, for instance, the State exercises power through the surveillance that is now possible because of the increased capacity to store information in the form of files and records. The knowledge that is available to those with access to or control over those sources enables them to predict, target and manipulate the behaviour of large numbers of people. These techniques are also at work in the agricultural world through, for instance, the computerization of accounts, details of what feed and drugs have been administered to stock, amounts of chemicals used on crops in specific fields and so on. Those unfamiliar with recent changes in agriculture underestimate the extent to which it is now, for the larger enterprises at least, a highly technical and rationalized business. This, of course, extends to control over the labour force, although with increasing mechanization, this is a less significant part of the operation.

However, even this does not fully capture the way that power was exercised in the locality. With the ownership of land and the subsequent control over employment and property went an authority that local people found very difficult to challenge. An outsider might interpret this as simply fear—fear of losing one's job and one's home—but there was more to it than this. Perhaps the only way to describe it is as a form of psychological dependence. Standing up to the local landowner in public would represent a challenge to a patriarchal and hierarchical social structure; almost like killing the father figure. To have done this would have taken some doing, particularly when there was no obvious system to replace it with. At least the familiar structure provided some security at a time when other factors, notably the influx of newcomers, were threatening the very fabric of community life.

This attitude is still deeply embedded, particularly among the older generation. Schoolteachers, doctors and ministers were treated with a deference and respect that had long since vanished in other parts of the country, because they too held a high position in the social hierarchy. Perhaps we need to add to Giddens' analysis a further category: power derived from the safety of a parental model of social relationships, which automatically accords to some people an authority that it is psychologically dangerous to threaten. Newcomers, eager to push forward changes that might also benefit local people, found themselves up against this almost intangible barrier.

So much then for a discussion of the sources of power. It is clear that it is valuable to be able to combine sociological and psychological insights. There is, however, another question about the nature of power that may further illuminate the local experience. Is power something that is possessed by individuals by virtue of their control over resources or is it, rather, a feature of institutions and structures? This tension was neatly encapsulated by Karl Marx when he said that men make history, but not in circumstances of their own making. To what extent are individuals in control over their own destinies and to what extent are they subject to forces beyond their control, such as bureaucratic structures and economic forces?

What sort of answer we give to this question is very important for the ways in which we conduct social and political life. For instance, there were certainly times when it felt as though the battles to retain local facilities such as schools and hospitals, were being waged against an impersonal force over which nobody really had any control. One of the ways in which bureaucracies work is to constantly shift responsibility from one department to another. You end up feeling that you can never deal with a fellow human being, but that everybody involved, including those within the relevant institution, are trapped in an insane maze of rules and regulations from which one can never escape. If this is what you then believe about where power lies it means that the only way to bring about change is to overthrow or reform these structures. There is no point trying to deal with the individuals employed there.

A good example of this was the struggle to put the house owned by the school trustees mentioned earlier into the rented housing sector. As you will recall from the previous section, restrictions and regulations promulgated by a number of different organizations were overcome because we discovered individuals with whom we could conduct regular and reasonable conversations. We were fortunate that the operation was humanized in this way, but, in many instances, this does not happen and people never find a way of coping with the institutional jungle.

It is certainly often the case that those struggling to effect change feel that their battle is somehow being waged against impersonal forces in these organizations over which no humans have much, if any, control. Yet, it is fellow humans who have devised and run these systems. The value of Giddens' approach to power is that it allows for due recognition to be given to both individual *and* institutional elements. That is, human beings are knowledgeable agents capable of effecting change, but they are also subject to forces working behind their backs over which they have little or no control. Thus, working for change means operating at both levels: establishing human contact *and* being aware of the organizational constraints within which they work.

There is sometimes a tendency to view power as automatically a bad thing, possibly because it is believed to be inherently coercive and to imply conflict. Giddens, however, tries to show that it is more appropriate to understand it as an integral element in all social life. Power is the human capacity to transform situations. Thus, it is necessary to bring about reforms, even though it can also be an agent of repression. This would seem to match the theological interpretations of people like Niebuhr and Tillich who point out the ambiguities of power. Power does not automatically entail violence. As Giddens says, it is both constraining and enabling. The real issue, though, is that of *how* power is to be used and *who* is to benefit from its use.

Does this mean, though, that even those who are apparently powerless have the capacity to change situations? Once again, local experience raised this question in very practical forms. There were times when those of us who had put time and effort into the community projects became frustrated and disheartened by the locals' unwillingness to carry their share of the tasks. Was this just a lack of self-confidence or was it that they really could not be bothered to do things for themselves? It sometimes felt as if those from the area who had any get up and go had long since got up and gone, and that those left behind were content with things as they were, even though they might complain about them. Perhaps they *did* have the power to bring about change, but not the initiative or the courage to do so.

This is where Giddens' approach can be misleading. He talks about a dialectic of control, within which the weak always have the capability to turn resources back against the strong, but an agent who has no options is no longer an agent at all. In theory this seems logical enough, but in practice the risks and dangers of trying to use even such limited power can be so great that one is effectively rendered powerless. I believe that this is a more accurate way of understanding the position of local, working-class families. If you have a family to support and no realistic alternative sources of housing or employment, it is not sensible to launch a challenge against your landlord and employer, even on such an important issue as the provision of housing for local people—that has to be left to those who are relatively independent of the local power structures and have less to lose. Giddens may be right in principle in saying that the power is available, but it is also true that it can, none the less, be impossible to utilize because of other constraining factors.

The next stage of the argument is to describe inappropriate and unjust uses of power. When does power become domination and when does domination need to be challenged? The classic answer to this is that when people are forced to act against their own best interests, power is being used unjustly and must be opposed. For instance, one might say that, in the case of a local teenager who was having to drive a tractor back to Shropshire from mid-Wales in the early hours of the morning, having worked since dawn the previous day, and who drove into a ditch when he fell asleep at the wheel, this person was being exploited because there was no other work for him. In this and other cases, the disparity of power is such that people are forced to follow courses of action that conflict with their own best interests. This is to deny a basic human freedom and dignity, to treat a fellow human being merely as a means to an end, as less than human.

If power is ever to be challenged, therefore, there must be some such basis on which that challenge can be made. The alternative is to leave things as they are. Political sociology would call this searching for a justification for an 'ideology critique', a means of identifying instances where it is appropriate to oppose current uses of power. However, this is not as straightforward as it might sound as it begs the question of whether people are always capable of knowing what is in their own best interests. To return to the case of the young tractor driver, this teenager was quite happy to take such risks, even though there were other members of his family who had suffered permanent injury because of similar incidents. One could say that he was young and enthusiastic, even irresponsible. He had no wife or children to consider and thoroughly enjoyed his work. Yet, because he refused to see the possible long-term consequences of the risks he was being forced to take he was prepared to be exploited. A full-blown ideology critique would aim to raise a person's awareness of the injustice of their situation in order that they be able to see where their true interests lie. It is a matter of controversy whether such a critique is possible.

There is another important contemporary interpretation of the nature of power that throws such an endeavour into question. As we said earlier, it is crucial to be aware of other perspectives if we are not to fall into the trap of an uncritical acceptance of one particular stance. Returning to the debate about whether it is individuals or structures that possess power, a third possibility has been suggested by the French philosopher, Michel Foucault.[4] In what he describes as an 'analytics of power', he proposes that power is not something that is *possessed* at all; it belongs neither to individuals nor structures because it is not that sort of a thing. Power is more like the air that we breathe, it is part of the nature of the relationships in which we live. It is unthinkable that there should not be power, but, instead of trying to identify who possesses it, we should try to isolate networks of power, specific points where it can be seen in operation. Like Nietzsche before him, Foucault believed that all knowledge is always already wrapped up in such power networks. If this is correct, it is a very important insight. It is supported by the example of military research that has been the basis for so many important technical and scientific advances. The search for knowledge is always backed up by interests in retaining or extending power.

While such an understanding is illuminating, it leaves us with the problem of not being able to make the sort of judgements necessary for an ideology critique. There is no way in which one can identify what is in somebody's best interests.

Foucault says at one stage that there is only power and counter-power and that there is no basis on which one can say that it is justifiable to replace one way of exercising power with another. If, for instance, one were to attempt to overthrow the power of the landed gentry in rural areas, it would only be replaced by another network that was neither better nor worse than the original.

Power, then, it would seem, is not something that some possess and some do not, but, rather, a strategy in which the dominated are as much a part of the network as the dominant. It is more important to find the *locus* of power than ask *what* power is. Beyond power is only more power and, thus, all attempts at emancipation and liberation are simply a shift from one power base to another. With this in mind, Foucault went on to analyse how power operated at a local level in ordinary everyday practices, including medical institutions and prisons.[5] This is the type of analysis that I have been trying to utilize within a local theology.

Foucault's approach has an obvious appeal, both because of its attention to local detail and because, like Giddens' work, it is realistic about the ambiguities of power. Within the local history group we became aware of how little had really changed, despite our efforts at community work. As far as local people were concerned, the power structures were what they ever were and all the self-confidence in the world was not going to change the fact that a few powerful families continued to be the dominant influences regarding employment and housing. The only way to change this would be to overthrow the feudal structure entirely—always a violent and bloody operation and one that merely leaves a power vacuum to be filled by others. There is only power and counter-power after all.

In the Parish Council or PCC, changes only came about as a result of a power struggle in which one group or individual took the place of another. Even the fashionable talk in church circles about devolving power to the laity has a certain hollow ring to it as *somebody* must have that power in order to be able to devolve it, and so is always in a position to take it back again should the experiment backfire. However, there is a real danger of becoming ultra-cynical if we follow Foucault through to this logical conclusion. As Christians we would surely want to hold on to the idea of being able to establish a base for an ideology critique, to find a way of discerning inappropriate and unjust uses of power.

Before I try to draw up a framework that might serve the purposes of a local theology, there is one more contribution to the debate that I want to examine. This comes from the work of Claus Offe, a German sociologist. In one of his books he attempts to show why it is that, despite democratic political structures, there are still glaring inequalities in Western society.[6] Although, in theory, we have equality of access to economic markets and the political process, in practice this is not the case. This, again, was borne out by my local experience. The mistake is to treat all groups as if they have the same starting point. For instance, the differences in the positions of groups within the class structure lead to differences in associational practice. In particular, the relatively powerless have to rely on creating a strong sense of collective identity in order to challenge the Establishment, as the history of the trade unions testifies. The powerful, however, can maintain their power merely by continuing to act individualistically and according to utilitarian and instrumental motives. Offe describes these as two different logics of collective action. In other words, those at the bottom of the pile have to fight in a different and more dangerous way in order to get a hearing. This has surely been the experience of women in recent years.

Protest also demands a public challenge in order to force power out into the open. You will recall that this is exactly what happened in the Parish Council when a local housing needs survey was debated. The problem, then, is that protesters are automatically labelled as troublemakers. No wonder, as they *have* to cause trouble in order to get a hearing.

They also have to go on the offensive and risk being seen as the aggressor, whereas those in possession of power only have to defend what they already have. The latter have the advantage, too, of being able to exercise their power behind the scenes where few ever see what is happening. Their power is largely hidden and dispersed, while that of the challengers must be open and concentrated in order to be effective. Each of these descriptions tallies exactly with our local experience.

Conclusion

It will be clear from what has emerged so far that there is a wealth of material available to aid in this process of trying to reach an understanding of the nature of power. I have only attempted to offer some of the work that seemed to be particularly illuminating in the local context. At each stage it can be seen how the ideas of thinkers such as Giddens, Foucault and Offe contribute to and highlight certain aspects of our own efforts to analyse and respond to the problems that we faced. No one framework is ultimately satisfying, but they provide shafts of light, thrown from different angles.

I will, however, offer some final thoughts on the subject in an attempt to draw together the various threads of the argument. The first thing to say is that it seems valuable to interpret power as a potential, something that is not always realized. When it is, it can be for better or worse; there is always an ambiguity involved. There are occasions when some groups or individuals gain from changes, but often only at the expense of others. It is not possible to know in advance the outcome of proposed changes, simply because there are always the unintended consequences of action, as Giddens pointed out. We are not entirely in control of either ourselves or our environment and we have to accept the risks involved in pressing forward into unknown territory. However, this is no reason to do nothing.

It may be helpful to view this human capacity to shape the future within given constraints along two axes. One possibility is that individuals or groups can use power to retain or gain control over others. If this is the case, then we have to ask whose interests are being served, acknowledging that it is often those who have the power who will benefit most from it. If there is clear injustice, exploitation and domination, then a challenge to this power is an appropriate response. On the other hand, power can be used to release greater control to others. This will not automatically be beneficial, but, normally, it is more appropriate to treat others as fully human and empower them to take greater control over their own lives. Along this axis, the burden of proof must be on those who wish to retain power over others to show that this, rather than its alternative, is of real benefit.

The other axis is that of change. Power can be used to keep things as they are. Once again, this is not automatically a bad thing—it depends on the nature of the particular status quo. Power can be used, however, to bring about change, given our awareness of the limited control we exercise over this process. The question remains, who will benefit from this and at what cost to others? Normally, it is those working for change who are attempting to improve life, so the burden of proof must be on those who are resisting it to show that *their* way is better. This must not be confused with the deterministic, evolutionary view that there is automatic progress for the human race or creation, it is merely a comment on the way things often turn out.

If we require a Christian rationale for this, it can surely be found in the example of Christ, whose attitude towards power was that it should be released for the benefit of those in need and expressed in a commitment to the other that entailed laying down his own power. His teaching on the kingdom of God also encourages us to keep moving forwards in hope towards a more just and peaceful social order, however distant and unreachable the final goal. Both of these factors support the notion that power is something to be shared for the benefit of all and that it is to be used to work towards a different future, a new creation.

Notes

1 Richard Lewis and Andrew Talbot Ponsonby, eds, *The People, the Land and the Church*. Diocese of Hereford, 1987.
2 Paul Tillich, *Love, Power and Justice*. Oxford University Press 1954. Reinhold Niebuhr, *Moral Man and Immoral Society*. SCM Press 1963.
3 Anthony Giddens, *A Contemporary Critique of Historical Materialism* (Macmillan 1981), pp. 61–3.
4 See Afterword by Michel Foucault in Hubert L. Dreyfus and Paul Rabinow, *Michel Foucault: Beyond Structuralism and Hermeneutics*. Harvester Press 1982.
5 Michel Foucault, *Discipline and Punish*. Peregrine 1979.
6 Claus Offe, *Disorganized Capitalism* (Polity Press 1985), Chapter 7.

2

The Meaning of Community

Introduction

Now to a discussion of community, as it was conflict over the possible meaning of this concept that underpinned the encounter with those on the margins. For instance, if we aimed to build new houses for local people, how should we define 'local'? How long should an individual or family have lived in the area before they could qualify for such housing provision? Also, we based our intervention in the housing debate on the assumption that it was important to retain a particular type of community, one in which there could be a balance between locals and newcomers, young families and the more elderly. How might it be possible to justify such an assumption?

Although these particular issues arose within a very specific context, many of them are encountered in other settings. One important reason for avoiding the descriptions 'rural' and 'urban' as much as possible is that it would disguise the fact that the same economic and social forces are at work throughout this country, they just manifest themselves in different ways given local circumstances.

What pattern of social relationships should we be working towards in this country, given the changes caused by capitalism and industrialization? If it is possible to answer this, then we can go on to decide to what extent current social life and, indeed, political policies facilitate or hinder such a vision. This is of particular interest to Christians as we assume that we have something to say about this area of human relationships. Quite what needs to be carefully examined.

Local questions of community

The clearest manifestation of this subject arose from within the context of tensions between locals and newcomers. This will be familiar to all who have lived in rural areas, but it happens elsewhere also. For example, in parts of cities subject to gentrification, where long-standing inhabitants find themselves living next door to young couples with a car each and other obvious trappings of success. This pattern—the more affluent moving to newly fashionable and desirable areas—has been common for well over a century. Cities such as Manchester have witnessed waves of successful business-people moving further away from the city centre in successive generations until, today, many are right out in the country-side, well away from their places of work. Parts of the city that were once considered desirable are now known as problem areas. A similar pattern applies with some immigrant groups in places such as London and Bristol. Particular parts of the city, perhaps close to the docks, have been the starting point for new groups from overseas, until they too become more affluent and move up-market, allowing the next group to move in.

The current situation in the countryside is just one more part of this wide pattern of social mobility. Some rural areas have no real local people left. There is no property available for rent or within their price range and probably no work either. The retired and the commuters have taken over and their life-styles, requirements and attitudes to community, including the local church, reflect an urban or suburban approach. One of the fascinating aspects of life in south-west Shropshire is that the process has not yet gone this far.

One of the valuable contributions made by our Local History Group was that it enabled some of us, inevitably deeply implicated in the changes that were happening, to stand back and reflect on them. For instance, it became clear early on that the locals and newcomers were not using the word community in the same way. As far as the former group were concerned, community was largely a thing of the past. There had already been so many changes, due to the impact of the Second World War, the increasing industrialization of agriculture and successive waves of newcomers, that the communities they had once known had ceased to exist. This contrasted with the expectations of many of the newcomers, who had moved to the country precisely to discover a sense of community life. Their comparisons were made with life in towns and cities, which seemed large-scale and, thus, impersonal.

As discussions in the Group progressed, it emerged that none of the newcomers, including myself, would want any part of the old-style 'community' described by the locals. For one thing it was oppressive, with so little freedom of choice, let alone resources, available to most of the population. If things seemed bad now, they were even worse then. However, it is in exactly such circumstances of hardship and deprivation that people have to bond together more in order to survive and that there is a stronger 'community spirit'.

It was because of this that local people were so ambivalent about the past. The pattern of social relationships seemed preferable to the present because it drew people closer together, but, at the same time, they were more than happy to have seen the back of some of the appalling living conditions that went with them. They were not about to idealize the past, yet they were also aware that some things had changed very little in practice. Local power structures were no different at all: the same families still owned most of the land and the tied farm workers' cottages, and were in a position to dictate terms to the working class. In this sense, the better living conditions were a mask for continued lack of freedom and self-determination.

This perhaps was the greatest source of tension. Many newcomers could not grasp that local people were still in the grip of this feudal system—they, after all, had *chosen* to live here. They might well be aware of the problems of lack of facilities, the threats to local schools and hospitals and the lack of public transport, but for them this was a trade-off for other things they wanted, notably community life. They were not dependent on the local landowners for work, property and patronage. They had taken choice for granted and, above all, they could choose to move out again if it did not work.

The local people in the Group were angry at the lack of awareness of their much more limited freedom. Their only choice would be to move right away from the area, leaving family and friends behind. In any case, this would mean going on a waiting list for a council property somewhere in the West Midlands conurbation. The prospects of finding somewhere to live this way are now somewhat slim. Then, what work would there be for them? Most had experience only of agricultural or related occupations—not exactly skills greatly in demand in the middle of Wolverhampton. Those who had chosen to leave the area had done so in previous generations when opportunities were better. So, what choice was there?

A second aspect of this tension between the two groups centred on their different patterns of work and social relationships. For most local people, this area is where they work and where their extended families live, so the whole fabric of their lives depends on the well-being of this geographical locality. This is not the case for newcomers. Many work out of the immediate area and, for the vast majority, family and friends are in other parts of the country. This makes a tremendous difference to attitudes towards the local community. Newcomers belong to networks spreading out beyond the locality and can satisfy some of their community requirements outside it. The farming fraternity, in some cases, also had contacts in other parts of the country and abroad. They belonged to another network.

The Meaning of Community

As part of his work for the second rural consultation, Richard Lewis, then the Agricultural Chaplain for the Diocese, drew up a pattern of the networks for the various groups and what emerged was a complicated web of relationships. The best way to describe this is as a series of spider's webs, but with lots of broken threads as well as unexpected connections. We tend to have this image of a rural community as one, coherent, clearly identifiable 'web', where everybody knows everybody else. This is just not true. Instead, there is a series of fragments, not a neatly bound, self-contained community.

In my own group of parishes one could identify a number of fragments. The local gentry; the larger tenant farmers and those in agricultural services; retired newcomers, often business people or from the Armed Forces or the colonial service; newcomers with young families, some working in the area but most commuting; a few professionals, doctors and teachers; the remnants of a wave of 'Good Lifers' from the 1960s and 1970s, those who had survived and integrated or formed their own network; and local, working-class people living in tied cottages or council properties with families in the area. Where did the local church draw its support from? Mostly from the first three categories.

It was impossible, therefore, to claim that the church was at the heart of community life. In fact, community life has no one focus at all in this context. Each local organization is no more than one fragment. Perhaps in the old days, when local society was a monochrome and hierarchical structure, there was a coherent community and the Church of England could claim to be at the heart of it, but only because it was identified with the upper echelons of the structure. Now that this pattern of social relationships has been broken, the only option seems to be to live within the fragments.

If this is the case, then what do we mean by 'community'? No one within the group seemed to have an answer for this. We felt we knew what it was in the past, but very few really wanted to return to that. Neither were we clear how one could foster close personal relationships in this setting where there were so many different networks and interest groups, or, indeed, whether that would be a good thing if it meant restricting freedoms and individual choice? Here we found ourselves at the very centre of the contemporary political debate about the conflict between liberal and socialist or collective values and I will expand on this shortly.

One helpful approach in this confusing situation is to ask how different groups elsewhere are using the word community. In particular, does it merely disguise a set of values and interests that are being imposed on others because we all agree that 'community' is a good thing? Even here the issue is not always clear cut and I will now give one more local example of this.

There were two primary schools in the group of parishes. In the village where I lived, and where my own three children went to school, the numbers were reasonably safe—in the mid fifties at that time. I was a governor of the school as well as being the Vicar and a parent. In the other school, numbers were falling to around the twenty mark and closure was threatened. I was the Chairman of Governors of this school and the Vicar. Part of the pre-closure consultation process for this school involved a discussion of where parents would like their children to go if the school were to close. I had a vested interest in encouraging parents to opt for the other school in my charge, although I knew that many had serious misgivings about it, but my argument was that it would keep the community together.

Needless to say, my arguments were challenged by parents and parent-governors. Their main concern was to obtain the best education possible for their children. If this meant going to other schools, then that was far more important to them than anything I could say about the value of community. I had to acknowledge that, if I was a parent at that school, I too would opt for the best education. I also had to own that I was using the word community ideologically, to disguise my vested interest as the Vicar.

However, there was a possible cost to the poorer parents attached to allowing the principle of individual choice to determine the outcome. The more affluent parents could afford to transport their children to a school of their choice regardless of the decision, and might well choose to do anyway, but the poorer parents, totally dependent on the provision of transport by the Education Authority, would have no such option: their children would have to go to the school for which transport was provided. The implication was that the parents would stand much less of a chance of gaining representation on the governing body of an alternative school unless they all agreed on the same option. Given the vital role that they had played in the present school, that seemed like a sad and regrettable loss of power. Had they opted for a merger with another school they could have retained much more say over its running, so, the position was not straightforward.

There is no doubt that the word community can have strong ideological overtones and that these always need to be identified in a particular debate. However, there is a real conflict beneath the surface between the principle of individual freedom of choice, and the power and opportunities that can come from some solidarity within social relationships. It is especially important for those with little power and limited say over policy decisions to stand together, but will those with greater power choose to stand with them as well? Here is a deep dilemma for local Christians. Once oppressive and restricting communities have been left behind and the freedom to exercise greater choice in one's own life has been gained, one is free to choose to ignore the needs of others. Many who 'make it good' from poor backgrounds would not dream of going back to stand in solidarity with those who have not been so fortunate. What values would need to be advocated to encourage those with power either to forego it or share it with others?

Political approaches to community

It is clear that the very word 'community' covers a range of meanings and is used in a variety of ways. About the only thing that can be said with any degree of certainty is that it is always talked about as being a good thing, even if it is only used to express an ideal. As a description, it could be used to refer to a number of social groupings. For instance, a geographical locality, an interest group, a system of solidarity, or a group with a sense of mutual significance or who share a moral viewpoint, set of beliefs, authority or ethnic identity. There are also occupational and purely functional groups as well as those who share a tradition. Which of these might be being commended when the word community is used?[1]

As if this is not confusing enough, we have to grapple with three separate political stances on the subject. Marxism embodies an ambivalence about community life. On the one hand, it works to see the back of all feudal structures, which prevent the emergence of the revolutionary class, and, yet, the very solidarity it seeks to foster in its place appears either hopelessly idealistic or else indistinguishable from the feudal pattern it seeks to banish. It has no real solution to offer regarding the question of what community would be like in a post-capitalist, socialist Utopia.

The conservative view values social order and a strict hierarchy in which everybody knows their place and is bound together by an ethic of mutual service and obligation. It was within this type of social structure that the Church of England found its natural home in previous generations, hence the strong emotional ties between the two powers in rural areas that still tend to be what we may call old-fashioned conservative. If one believed in social inequality, this system could undoubtedly be of benefit to those lower down the social scale. However, one can no longer choose to live community this way, even if it *could* be justified, given the fragmentation that has now taken place.

Finally, there is the liberal stance, which views the decline of community as the opportunity for individuals to free themselves from the shackles of a hierarchical society and to become consuming, exchanging, and contracting people within the market-place. Community is often equated with coercion and the imposition of values and ways of life that are unacceptable in a pluralistic society. There may be partial or voluntary communities based on co-operation and altruism, but these will not be capable of meeting the needs of those who do not fit in. This is the classic dilemma that was outlined earlier in this chapter and which now looms so large in a country that has been governed for over a decade according to liberal individualistic values. Community is not something that should be legislated for or taken account of in political policy. If this happens, it is just a lucky bonus, but it is not the basis on which to run an economy.

It is obvious from these descriptions which is the current, dominant, political ideology. It has to be acknowledged that its understanding of contemporary Britain matches our own very closely. We no longer have a feudal hierarchy, nor do we have anything like a socialist Utopia. There is no such thing as society or, indeed, community. What we have are different interest groups competing for scarce resources on the open market and it is not the legitimate role of government to intervene in this negotiation.

As with the example of the primary schools, what this disguises is the fact that, in this so-called open market, some groups are automatically in a stronger bargaining position than others. If there are legitimate obligations towards those with less power, this must have implications for the legislative and political structures. Otherwise, only the strongest and fittest will survive, which is what has been happening for the last decade or more. Such a one-sided interpretation of the liberal tradition is, in effect, an ideological ploy to limit the benefits of capitalism to those already in power. This is like feudalism in different clothing.

Let us switch direction here. We need to examine another set of options that have, so far, been quietly ignored, even by the church, which is supposedly searching for another way forward. The spectre of a socialist Eastern Europe in political and economic decay, combined with its oppressive regimes, has come to discredit all socialist policies in the public mind. Put crudely, socialism and freedom are seen as mutually exclusive and, during a time of rapid change and uncertainty, we do not feel generous towards experimentation. As a result, social relationships have become fragmented and the worship of the individual at the expense of the collective has been encouraged. If this is true, then what is required is a version of socialism that while honouring what is best in the liberal tradition, creates a political framework that fosters community life, or more appropriate social relationships.

Much thought and debate in this area has centred on the role of the Welfare State. The argument from the New Right has been that high levels of State intervention have discouraged the individual initiative and enterprise so essential for a healthy economy. Investment and, indeed, the will to succeed have been eroded by over-taxation to fund welfare services. There is a genuine conflict here that has not always been duly acknowledged by socialists. The objective of accumulation of capital is not served by the aims of the Welfare State at any time. However, most socialist policies have attempted a compromise between the two and this has led to the fear of loss of freedoms that has worked so powerfully in the Conservatives' favour.

Is there not a third way, though, that neither pursues accumulation of capital at the expense of the less powerful in society, nor returns us to the over-bureaucratized and often ineffective Welfare State of the 1960s and 1970s?

The future of community

In order to discover if there is a way of establishing a pattern of social relationships that does not inhibit individual freedom, we need to examine some ideas from the discipline of political sociology. In particular, it is helpful to utilize the distinction between 'the State' and 'civil society'. By the latter we are to understand areas of life that are not directly under the control of government, for instance, households, voluntary organizations and community-based services. What are the prospects, in this context, for community life?

The New Right argue that one of the problems of socialism is that it encroaches too deeply into civil society. However, if one looks at the evidence of the last decade in this country, it is clear that this is not exclusively a socialist weakness. Despite its rhetoric about rolling back the powers of the state, the Conservative government has consistently intervened in other areas of public and private life. Even now, voluntary organizations are facing new regulations about levels of staffing and training for volunteers that will make operating them more costly and difficult. Attempts to hand power back to consumers of education and health care only end up producing more centralized bureaucratic control and adversely affecting the provision of services to poorer sections of the community.

What the New Right has done is to emphasize one set of virtues required by civil society at the expense of another. It has advocated self-interest, hard work, self-reliance, freedom of choice, private property, the patriarchal family and a distrust of state bureaucracy. These need to be counterbalanced by the virtues needed for better social relationships, such as a concern for others, a willingness to share resources, a sense of the common good and a concept of civic responsibility. If this is not done, then society is basing itself on an inadequate understanding of what it is to be a human being, which reduces the individual to a passive consumer, valuable only as the subject of commercial interests.

What is required is a new definition of the relationship between the State and civil society. Groups and organizations operating in the latter need to be given a framework that will enable more people to participate in their activities. At the same time, the state must be made more accountable to its citizens. In this way, the boundaries between government and other bodies can be clearly drawn while acknowledging that the two are interdependent. As John Keane says:

> . . . without a secure and independent civil society of autonomous public spheres, goals such as freedom and equality, participatory planning and community decision making will be nothing but empty slogans. But without the protective, redistributive and conflict-mediating functions of the State, struggles to transform civil society will become ghettoized, divided and stagnant, or will spawn their own, new forms of inequality and unfreedom.[2]

How will this contribute to the fashioning of a new kind of community life? I think we have to acknowledge that it is not possible to deliberately set out to create community. What *can* be done, however, is to create an environment in which close relationships are more likely to flourish. Unfortunately, recent government actions have made it clear that this is not seen as a valid task. Its only interest in civil society has been as an alternative provider of services that can then enable it to eliminate areas once covered by the Welfare State.

We now need to establish a definition of community, therefore, that has a direct bearing on our fragmented and pluralist society. What sort of relationships are possible now that the old style of community has disappeared? Anthony Black talks about the experience of 'communio', and I believe that this is a helpful contribution.

> By communio I mean a feeling of togetherness which people can experience in relatively small groups. It falls short of full comradeship but is intenser than friendly acquaintance. This is a personal relationship in that

communio arises only among individuals who know each other personally. Like the relationships communio is subjectively meaningful and valued for itself; it enhances peoples' lives independently of other advantages which group or community membership may bring.[3]

Black believes that such a feeling of community can never be guaranteed in any social group—it is more likely to occur as an unintended consequence of other activity. This seems to be borne out by experience. Those who set out to create community seem doomed to disappointment while groups that aim to perform entirely different functions are often the places where these sorts of relationships flourish. A Neighbourhood Watch scheme, for instance, can serve as a catalyst in one area but get no response whatsoever in another.

If this is the case, then it reinforces Keane's approach of establishing opportunities within which community will be more likely to happen and not setting out to force it into existence. This may mean trying to break down barriers that inhibit the growth of community. We need to know under what circumstances it is possible for people to meet and work together in this informal manner. There needs to be a common cause and motivation but also time and space. Other recent changes in social life are making the latter two increasingly difficult to find. In particular it must be recognized that women have played leading roles in much voluntary work in the past, but, now, more women are seeking full-time paid employment, so fewer are available for or willing to become volunteers. We must beware of making the sexist assumption that women will provide a consistent source of informal labour.

There are two possible solutions to this. One is to guarantee everybody a minimum annual salary, regardless of hours or conditions of employment. This might then release both men and women who want to engage in voluntary activity. This goes against the ethos of all the political parties who still equate 'work' with full-time, productive, paid employment.

The second is to move towards a more radical understanding of what tasks are productive for society and to value what are, at the moment, low-status, informal and often voluntary activities. Given current economic pressures, unless there is such a change of perspective, one can see that there will be fewer people being prepared to offer their time to community life—they will require all the time and space available to them merely to survive.

What other factors are working against better forms of social relationship? There is a well-established argument in sociology about the changes resulting from the growth of large-scale urban and industrial environments. According to this, people are alienated from each other and an atmosphere of mistrust and even hostility prevails. The strong ties of family and close relationships characteristic of pre-industrial and rural society are replaced by more functional and impersonal relationships. If this is accurate, then it is not likely that people will be willing to overcome their fears and engage in community activity.

As Giddens has pointed out, this is to overstate the case. It is more accurate to say that relationships have *changed* rather than that they have broken down altogether. For example, with the advent of modern communications technology, it is now possible to create and sustain personal relationships beyond one's immediate geographical locality. This was clearly part of the tension between locals and newcomers in Shropshire, where the latter often belonged to social networks that had nothing to do with the area. The new aspect of such relationships is that they are built on an intimate but tenuous trust. People are not bound together by kinship or even economic necessity, but by a positive, personal commitment to others with whom there may be only irregular face-to-face contact. Such ties are inevitably more risky and require a willingness to remain open to the other at a deeper level that is unnecessary when there is a concrete local structure for the relationships. This new dimension needs to be taken into account in future discussions about community.[4]

A further factor invariably associated with community lfe is the question of scale. It seems undoubtedly true that the larger the number of people involved in a particular group or enterprise, the harder it becomes to sustain close, personal relationships. This is presumably the major reason for rural life being seen, still, as a haven of community. The scale of relationships can remain more manageable and it is at least feasible to know most of one's fellow inhabitants in a village. 'Small is beautiful' appears to be an inescapable maxim, even where networks are concerned. In which case, it remains important to be able to encourage the growth of small, if not necessarily locally based, groups. More positive support by means of funding is sometimes an appropriate way for government and, indeed, the church to facilitate such groups.

Finally, we need to come full circle and consider how the local church might contribute to better social relationships. It has the immediate advantage of being small scale and local, but this has not necessarily provided an appropriate framework for community. In fact, there is a tendency for local churches to become exclusive social groups rather than offering space for *all* to participate. A first priority must be for Christians to be prepared to go out into the various fragments of local society and work alongside those who are excluded— not in order to convert them, but to express its commitment to those in need. Second, it should be prepared to use its power at the local level to push for the political changes that would provide a greater security for civil society. Third, it must work towards a deeper understanding of the relationships of trust that now seem to be the basis for future community life. Finally, it needs to offer a model of relationships that can allow for difference and conflict. If market forces are not to be the only arbiter of conflicting interest groups within society, there must be an alternative model. If this cannot be found, then only the powerful and successful will thrive, and this seems to contradict a Christian concern for the whole of creation.

The process that began with specific, localized issues has led on here to a more detailed and varied discussion, drawing on the resources of sociology and political studies. They show that there is a need for systematic consideration of the questions if there is to be an adequate response to what are, inevitably, wider problems of social relationships.

Notes

1 Raymond Plant, Harry Lesser and Peter Taylor-Gooby, *Political Philosophy and Social Welfare* (Routledge & Kegan Paul 1980), Chapter 9.
2 John Keane, *Democracy and Civil Society* (Verso 1988), p. 15.
3 Anthony Black, *State, Community and Human Desire* (Harvester Wheatsheaf 1988), p. 50.
4 Anthony Giddens, *The Consequences of Modernity* (Polity Press 1991), p. 115ff.

3

The Cultured Despisers
of Religion

Introduction

The major practical contact with those in the area who were
committed to the improvement in social conditions and yet
did not share a specific Christian faith was through our community projects, brought about by two groups: the Play
Scheme and Local History Group. The key question in this
part of the book is how it might be possible to discover ways
of working together at a local level that both reveal common
ground between Christians and other groups, and also
respect genuine differences. To fail in the first of these tasks
would mean isolation from others; to fail in the second would
risk turning conversation into colonization. Together, this
would represent a failure to do justice to the insights of our
faith community.

The idea that the local church should become involved in
community work has been around for some time. It was certainly talked about and put into practice a good decade ago
in urban areas such as Manchester. My encounter with this
way of working as a curate in that diocese was largely on a
theoretical level, looking at arguments about political
involvement and whether or not it was possible for members
of the established church to work *with* rather than *for* people.
The idea surfaced again more recently in discussions regarding

roles for the ordained ministry, with the proposal that the local clergy should operate on a community work model. So, the seeds had been sown in my mind some time back, but had not yet found ground in which they could begin to grow.

The discussions that had taken place in the Local History Group had led us to the conclusion that the church could no longer claim to be at the heart of community life, but was no more than one of the many fragments. It seemed from this that pastoral ministry had to entail working out in those fragments, making contact with those who would otherwise steer clear of official religion. To concentrate energy on building up the congregation would inevitably be a limiting enterprise, at worst creating another exclusive and unrepresentative social grouping.

In this shifting sand of social relationships, it seemed that the community work model might have something to offer. What needed to be recognized, though, was that community work in a scattered rural area could not take exactly the same form as in an urban setting. For instance, community workers attempting to set up support groups such as Gingerbread or Cruse soon discovered that there were not enough people in any one category in these remoter areas to form viable groups. When the population is so much smaller and often remote, single-interest groups of *any* nature are that much more difficult to sustain. The trick is to establish local groups that cover a variety of needs and interests and supply a community worker to enable and support them until they can survive alone.

Put simply, new forms of community require new methods of community work. I would agree with older members of the clergy who believed it was the task of the local church to be involved with the community, but I would maintain that, in order to do this effectively in changing social circumstances, there is a need to adopt and adapt urban styles of community work. The alternative is for the church to become increasingly inward-looking and congregationally based. It was with this sort of argument in the background that we became involved in a different way of working.

The play scheme

On the face of it, such a project hardly seems very radical. It is not easy to explain why this specific scheme became so important to our work in the locality. Perhaps some other focus would have emerged, but it just so happened that this one idea set off a chain of events—the seed from the poppy head landed in fertile ground. It is not possible to predict how apparently innocuous ideas can become crucial for this style of community development work. If there is a lesson embedded here, it is that it is essential to take the risk of following up superficially trivial suggestions because you can never know where they are going to lead.

This idea was cooked up one night in a local pub after a routine PCC meeting. It was not directly related to the church at all, although it required somebody in a leadership role to take some initial action. During discussion over a drink, it was noted that there was very little for children to do during the summer holidays. An important factor in this was geographical isolation. A large number of the children lived on outlying farms or in scattered hamlets, and, without transport or a meeting place, tended not to get together once school had finished for the summer. One of the younger fathers, who had only moved into the area fairly recently, but was already involved in the church and a member of the Local History Group, suggested that an obvious way of meeting this social need would be to set up a play scheme. We did not have a clue about what this would involve, but it seemed like a good idea.

If the first lesson is being prepared to follow up obscure ideas, the second is knowing who to contact for advice and resources. By this stage in the process we had worked long enough with the Rural Officer for the Community Council to know that if she did not know something she inevitably knew somebody else who did. This is the role of the facilitator. We discovered that play schemes were quite common community projects and that the Community Council had produced a pack on how to go about setting one up, based on their experiences elsewhere. It was wonderful not to have to reinvent the wheel as it were. It occurs to me that the church, with its tremendous wealth of local resources, has never really utilized them properly and rarely as helpfully as this. Perhaps most congregations are too insular, even competitive.

The next stage involved many informal discussions outside the school gates, in the village shop and anywhere else where we encountered people we thought might be interested in being involved. We wanted to see if the idea provoked a positive response, but we also wanted to gauge the level of personal commitment to the scheme. There is a lot to be said for floating ideas about over a long period of time so that they can become established in peoples' minds before it comes to the point of any firm action or decisions being taken. This was particularly important as we envisaged a locally run play scheme with the minimum of outside assistance. We wondered, would other young parents with a vested interest in having entertainment for their children during the summer be prepared to do some of the work?

It is significant that the leadership at this stage came from two men. In due course this raised questions about the role of women in the area and the general lack of confidence they displayed, particularly those who were local. As noted earlier, it has normally been women who have provided most volunteer labour for community projects, but the two men involved were fortunate enough to have jobs that allowed them the possibility of being around during the day to help with the scheme. The only others who could be available during the week were women who were working part-time or not working.

For all the members of the planning group, organizing a

project of this nature was a new experience and we found ourselves moving into unfamiliar territory. For instance, not only did we need to marshall the active support of other parents, but also had to think about venues, timing, provision of food, publicity, legal implications, and the raising of funds. There was much more to this than we had first anticipated. As with other community projects, so much of the value of the enterprise is the experience and confidence gained through tackling new ventures. Fundraising, in particular, we found to be a world of its own, where the prizes seem to go to those with the most initiative and who learn how to play the system most effectively. Once again, the advice from the Community Council was invaluable. They told us where financial support might be available and how best to present our project.

Part of the learning process involves developing new practical skills such as these that can then be employed in other situations. As this began to open up other horizons for those of us directly engaged in setting up the scheme, we also realized that here was an opportunity to benefit other sections of the local community. For instance, the play scheme would provide extra income for the village hall and for the local shop, with whom we opened an account. We also established an arrangement with the pub in the village to provide takeaway meals at lunchtime for those who did not want to bring packed lunches. This was all good business for local traders and fostered a sense of co-operation. In fact, at the end of the first year, the Village Hall Committee were so pleased that we had done something for the young people that it made only a minimal charge for the hire of the hall. However, we paid them extra as a donation because we had the outside funding and we appreciated how important their support had been. The play scheme became a way of oiling the wheels of community relationships in a manner that we had never envisaged. We had not set out to do this, but it was one of the wonderful consequences of the scheme.

Another aspect of this was that the play scheme enabled greater personal contact between locals and newcomers. Meeting the needs of the children provided a shared common interest and a relaxed atmosphere within which the adults, too, could mix and begin to learn more about each other. This happened when they would organize an activity together, but also in the casual conversations that took place over coffee and during lunch breaks. As we saw in Chapter 2, this is something that cannot be created artificially, but it is possible to establish an environment in which it is more likely to occur. It must also be said, however, that the tensions between the two groups were still there beneath the surface and continued to emerge in the familiar guise of locals resenting newcomers doing too much of the organizing. Such feelings seem to be inevitable, but perhaps the best to hope for is an atmosphere in which they can be aired freely so that these tensions are not allowed to disrupt the work itself.

There were two other significant spin-offs of the play scheme. The first was as a result of this growing awareness of the needs of young mothers in the area.

Towards the end of the first year of the play scheme, one of the mothers suggested setting up a ladies rounders team. Once again, this does not sound like a particularly radical idea, but it proved to be a significant step. It was a chance to be together for an evening, to leave the children with fathers or grandparents, to go for a drink after the game and for the women to have the kind of social activity previously only available to the menfolk. Here, in a small way perhaps, was a victory for women's liberation. The importance of such opportunities must not be underestimated. They are so often a vital part of the process of confidence-building, of gaining self-worth and the seedbed for other community activities.

The second new venture that stemmed directly from the play scheme was a Saturday morning football session for the primary school boys. This was set up and run by one of the fathers who was not able to be involved in the play scheme itself because he would be at work, but wanted to do something. Those living in more highly populated areas where it is easier to find enough children and adults to establish sports teams might not appreciate how difficult such projects are in remoter rural localities. The time commitment involved is considerable and for someone to come forward and offer this as his contribution to community life is a substantial response to local need.

The wider questions

Why should such schemes be seen as part of a local theology? Is this not just social or community work in which some Christians happen to have become involved? This could, indeed, be the case and such a level of involvement would be admirable and legitimate. In this particular instance, however, both the original impetus for and the subsequent developments as a result of the play scheme were the direct results of the growing awareness of local problems stemming from the activity of the Local History Group. The issue of community life and the recognition of lack of resources available to local people were part of the stimulus for the project. The process of critical reflection on local circumstances begun in that forum led to this particular practical response.

Community work has traditionally been associated with the Left in political terms because it involves empowering people to take greater control over their own lives and giving them the confidence to challenge authority where it is seen to be acting unjustly. In Christian terms we might talk about the restoration of dignity and self-worth and an approach that responds to God's love for us by trying to meet the needs of others. However, it is essential not to become romantic about community work and to set it in a wider political context.

We need to ask how community work is being used in the contemporary political climate. As soon as we do this, we can begin to see the ambiguities. With current government thinking striving to redefine the role of the Welfare State, community work and self-help groups generally fit neatly into a strategy that aims to throw as much welfare service as possible back into the voluntary sector. The provision of services is deemed to be the responsibility of the family, of local, informal, caring networks, of community agencies and voluntary bodies, such as local churches. The Welfare State will become a minimal structure, a safety net for those who slip through the grasp of the voluntary sector. This will allow central government to reduce basic rates of income tax and feed money back into the commercial sector.

In such a political climate, there is a real sense that the development of community projects is in some way an act of collusion with a strategy that is designed to undermine the Welfare State. Is this a position that Christians should be happy to adopt? My own belief is that there needs to be more of a balance between central and local funding of welfare services based on a vision that such services should still be available in equal measure to all, whatever their financial resources and wherever they happen to live.

Unless there is central funding and, thus, some subsidization for local services, they will cease altogether, as has happened many times already. Feeding money into small-scale local community projects, such as our play scheme, is not a substitute for the proper provision of services. However, this is the way such projects are viewed in the current political climate. The position we felt obliged to defend locally is that local and central provision should not be seen as alternatives, but, rather, be complementary parts of the same strategy. There should be both support for the local projects *and* an availability of central funding for welfare services. Along with this should go greater local control over the nature of these services and greater central protection of local community organizations. What we have at the moment is merely greater centralization of increasingly unavailable services.

There is, then, a deep conflict involved in local Christian community work. On the one hand, it represents a legitimate and worth while response to local needs, but, on the other, it appears to be collusion with an élitist approach to the provision of welfare services. In this situation, our responsibilities are surely both to continue to respond to these needs *and* to make it clear that this should not be happening at the expense of other sectors of society. It is part of the task of a local theology, then, to open up the debate about the future of the Welfare State and to enter into the sort of detailed political arguments suggested above. To do less would be to betray Christian visions of social justice.

Such conflict was highlighted by the comments of the father who had initially suggested the play scheme. He wondered if all that we had done by setting up our various projects had been to raise unrealistic expectations in the minds of local people. It had been the middle-class newcomers who had pressed for better services, but it was they who so often moved on when they realized that they were never going to obtain them in this beautiful, but remote and politically archaic valley. What about the local people who could *not* move on to better-serviced areas? They were still trapped and nothing substantial had changed for them. Had we just given them a glimpse of things that were forever out of their reach, or had we given them a start in being able to fight for better local services? In discussions within the group, we concluded that it was better to have done something than to have sat back and accepted the status quo, that we had to believe and have the hope that the process would bear fruit; to do nothing is worse than trying and failing. This seems to be an act of faith, a commitment to a way of working that remains risky and may lead nowhere. Perhaps we had begun to learn what hope actually means—one of those previously idealistic, theological words had come to life for us.

Is it appropriate, though, for a minister to play the role of a community worker in his or her area of responsibility? This local example would encourage a positive response to such a question. There is, undoubtedly, a leadership function projected on to clergy in this setting, so the question then is what *type* of leadership should be given? If Christian leadership involves vision, I would want to translate this as meaning seeing the possibilities in a particular situation. We learned this from our colleagues in the Community Council. They had the experience and the ability to come into an area and see very quickly what could be done, especially what people could do for themselves. This is an invaluable quality and should be fostered in ministers, as they are so rooted in local life.

Other words that spring to mind in connection with community workers are 'enabling', 'empowering', 'catalytic'. Local clergy are in a unique position in that they are often the only professionals residing in deprived areas. This is their patch, their area of responsibility, and it is their task to know and care for it. If Christianity has a vision of more just social relationships, then what better way to put it into action than through this type of involvement? This does not mean the old-style paternalistic methods of doing things *for* people, but of enabling people to do things for themselves—a much more subversive but positive process. It raises its own ambiguities, as we have seen, but, as we have also seen, an awareness of them is an essential part of the task and certainly no excuse for inaction. New patterns of community require new styles of community work and there is a need for Christians to be part of this experiment.

The Local History Group

It seems appropriate now to consider in more detail the nature and workings of the core group in the local area. The Group itself never adopted a particular name and it was referred to in a number of different ways by those involved. This was not a problem as identity or status were never issues for us. From the outset, a wide range of interests were covered and one of the keys to the operation was to prevent the Group becoming exclusive. The meetings took place over three years and numbers present ranged from six to twenty-six, depending on the scope of a particular meeting.

Although the local history work was the most important thread running through the Group, there was also some environmental content and discussion of matters of local and national politics. The early meetings tried to take up specific themes and invited speakers, but, latterly, we drew up our own agenda when the people actually met so that we could concentrate on immediate issues. The question that we will need to address shortly is what can be learned from this method of operation for the process of local theology, but before we move on to that it is important to clear away some possible misunderstandings.

The nature of the Group

Part of the problem in defining the nature of the Group is that it is difficult to find models that fit what we were doing. Perhaps the most obvious parallel comes from the church in Latin America and what are now known as 'basic Christian communities', or, 'base ecclesial communities'. I want to explain why such a description would not be appropriate.

The social context in Latin America is very different to our own. A speaker at a conference on basic Christian communities offered the following explanation of where they fitted into the wider context. Imagine a solar system such as our own. At the heart of it is the Sun. The Sun is the local priest, who is the focus for all local, institutionalized, religious activity. Around the Sun is a cluster of planets. These are the people intimately involved in the life of the local church and who look to the priest for leadership. Then there are a number of stray asteroids and other celestial bodies who, from time to time, cut through the orbits of these planets. These are the people who still have a vague connection with and attachment to the church, but who are only likely to encounter it at times of crisis or at baptisms, weddings or funerals. Beyond this solar system lies the rest of the universe. This is where the majority of people are and the model reflects the fact that religion rarely, if ever, touches their lives.

Basic Christian communities consist largely of people from the asteroid belts; those on the fringes of the church who can be drawn back into its orbit if religion can be made more meaningful for their particular circumstances. What liberation theology has done is to show that the Christian tradition can offer insights and encouragement in circumstances of rapid social change, which exacerbate existing oppression and tighten the grip of unjust social structures. There is, though, an inevitable tension between such grass roots movements and centralized church hierarchies. The gravitational pull is still towards the centre and the pressures on the fringe groups are to move closer to this and initiate gradual reforms. There has, perhaps, been a tendency in this country to see basic Christian communities as being more radical than this, based on the writings of some of the liberation theologians, but such a description does not fit this particular local theology project.

The Local History Group was never explicitly churchy or Christian—it contained regular members who were firmly within the 'solar system', those who could be described as being on the fringes of local church life, and some who were out in the wider 'universe', for whom the Christian tradition was problematic to say the least. To continue in the language of this image, the Group was right out on the edge of the 'solar system', encroaching into potentially hostile territory. Thus it could not be described as a basic Christian community.

There are a number of comments that can be made about this. First, this was where the Group needed to be in order to be effective. The local churches did not have the personnel with the skills to facilitate community projects such as the play scheme, but there were local non-church people who were interested in and willing to be involved. The main task was not to draw these individuals into the local church, but to establish projects in which Christians could find appropriate practical expressions of their faith by working alongside others with similar concerns. It provided the non-churchgoers with the opportunity to share, in open discussion, some of the deeper issues that arose. This was valuable for both groups.

In different contexts in this country it is possible that the model of the basic Christian community might be more workable. However, I think that one should be cautious about this. It does seem possible that, where there are ethnic communities with a strong Christian background, there will be significant numbers of fringe Christians who might be drawn back into the church if it can show that the tradition can speak to their situation. I do not believe that the same can be said for the rest of the population. While there are those who are on the fringes of church life in the sense that they may come into contact with it at times of crisis and so on, most of them do not now share the Christian cultural background of these ethnic communities. By this I mean that they are more thoroughly secularized, no longer familiar with patterns of biblical thought and Christian worship, so interpreting local situations in terms of biblical stories, for instance, is not going to be particularly useful. Their natural narratives may relate to explicitly local events—the closure of factories or schools, say, or the impact of the Second World War. Shared stories become even more problematic for those who have moved around the country or the world and have never been anywhere long enough to become part of a particular locality in this way. If they have natural narratives, they may be more personal, based on their family or on an individual's experiences. The way in which theology needs to be done, therefore, will vary according to social circumstances. The experience of the Local History Group was that

it required a more open and less explicitly Christian structure. We must beware of dismissing as non-theological or not
Christian enough modes of operation that do not conform to
a model that is derived from a very different social setting.

If we return to the sociological insights into this area of
south-west Shropshire offered earlier, it may become clear
why the Local History Group had to take the form it did. The
social structure of the area, you will recall, is fragmented.
One of the major problems is establishing any real contact
between the different fragments. If the local church can reasonably still be seen as a solar system in the locality—and that is
very much open to question—it is only one of a number of
competing solar systems. The whole analogy, in fact, appears
to break down in this context. It is far more helpful to view
local society as a series of networks, of which the church is
just one. In which case, if the church is to exercise a pastoral
ministry within the whole community, it needs to be present,
often through its individual members, in as many of these
other networks as possible. If it has a wider role, it can only
be as an inter-network network, providing a forum or some
common ground for other networks. It cannot do this if its
declared aim is to capture all the other groups within its
own net.

This has considerable implications for a local theology. The
alternative is either to set up explicit church groups designed
for bible study or prayer or whatever, which then merely
alienate other fragments, or to take up a more implicit stance
and reach out to other groups on the basis of shared local
concern and action. The debate is a familiar one. In the first
option, the church becomes a sect, hoping to influence society
from the outside. In the second, it risks its integrity and identity by becoming too involved with the world. Our local
experience led to the conclusion that this latter view is based
on a misunderstanding of the relationship between the
church and the world. The church is always *already* part of
the world, even if it likes to *think* of itself as being separate.

Both its structures and its individual members are as much influenced by economic and social forces as the rest of society. Failure to recognize this only leaves Christians open to political manipulation, divorces the spiritual from the material and decontextualizes theology. The *real* question that Christians need to address is that of how to enable their beliefs to make a real difference to this shared reality.

With this picture in our minds it becomes easier to see why the Local History Group developed such an open structure. There were no officers, no minutes, no constitution. The meetings were advertised well in advance so that anybody could attend, and it was known that this was not a *church* group. It attempted to offer a different experience of power from that at work in all other local organizations, including the church. At one stage, it was agreed that anybody could come to a meeting and have ten minutes to talk on any subject of their choice, either their particular interest or a burning issue that they wanted to raise. It seemed as though there was nowhere else that people could go in order to have a voice and be listened to—both essential ingredients in human integrity. It was also an opportunity to gain support from others, to know that one's concerns were taken seriously.

Perhaps here is a model for local democracy. If one accepts the description of society as a series of fragments, a plurality of different interest groups and, indeed, cultures, then the value that we would surely want to place on each of these as Christians can most obviously be put into practice through a structure that allows each group an equal voice. The patterns of democracy currently in place work *against* this, as social and economic power give advantages to specific groups. This became clear in the debate about local housing, for instance. Such power imbalances can only be redressed, in the first instance, by positive discrimination in favour of disadvantaged groups. If everybody started from the same position it would be different, but this is never the case, which is why it was so important to allow space for the sections of local society whose voices and stories were previously suppressed. Many rural churches have spent too much of their time listening to the accounts of their affluent and powerful supporters to have a balanced picture. Once this listening process had begun, stories began to emerge that otherwise could only be told indirectly through drama or literature. This led on to the practical responses described earlier that, in turn, enabled the discussion of deeper issues of morality and politics. It was then that the Christians in the group began to clarify what their beliefs contributed to the discussions and how they provided a basis for the local action. This is what local theology became in this specific context—a process of reflective engagement that brought certain aspects of the Christian tradition to life. For the first time, perhaps, we could begin to see what some of these words meant in the light of the very real problems we faced together.

I will expand on this process in the next chapter, but, first, let me just mention another dimension to this discussion of local theology. There has been much written in recent years about the way in which religion has become an increasingly private matter. Thus, for instance, worship often appears to be the province of lone individuals sitting quietly in their pew and leaving the church having received their spiritual 'fix' for the week. Religion is also seen as a form of psychological support for those going through periods of personal crisis, perhaps a bereavement or a divorce. The increasing interest in counselling appears to emphasize this personal dimension and could be criticized on the grounds that it is encouraging a passive, conformist attitude to wider social problems. At the other extreme, there are those who put all their Christian eggs into the basket of political activism and highlight the collective implications of faith. This division may well reflect a more widespread tendency to separate private and public life.

Local theology, however, cannot afford to fall wholly into

either of these camps and may, in fact, be able to show that this division is both unhealthy and unnecessary. On a practical level, Christians need to be able to show their concern for others in both individual *and* collective spheres. The Christian faith can be a source of hope and support for individuals in times of crisis, but it can, equally, offer both to groups in society who are struggling for greater justice. It is a 'both/and', not an 'either/or', although it may be necessary in some situations to give more emphasis to one in order to redress an existing imbalance.

We have seen how the encounters with non-Christian groups occurred in my locale. What they left me with were wider questions about how issues of faith can be related to those who do not share a specific religious commitment. This involves both a practical and a theoretical dimension. On the first level, Christians have to learn to work alongside those with whom they might have significant differences of opinion. The deeper question revolves around the impact of this work in terms of its content and the interpretations of the idea of a faith community. Will it require a rethinking of the claims that one makes for one's own tradition and the risk of a sell-out or compromise, or are there ways forward that can acknowledge the integrity of both sides in the discussions? The next chapter will examine such possibilities.

4

A Post-modern
Christianity

Introduction

The major concern of many traditional Christians with the description of the relationship between themselves and the cultured despisers of religion offered in the previous chapter will be that it undermines anything they would recognize as Christianity. What I want to suggest in this chapter is that this is not necessarily the case. The effect of this new approach is certainly to challenge any universal claims to authority, whether they be made by religion, science, philosophy or politics, but it does not follow from this that it is invalid to make substantial claims of any nature, nor that human beings are incapable of discriminating between the claims that are made. In this sense, there is no reason for Christians to stop putting forward their views and interpretations with any less conviction than anybody else. What is now required, though, is a greater willingness to be open and questioning about one's own position in order to give due recognition and respect to those with different views.

What I intend to do now is try to show that there are, in fact, significant and illuminating parallels between some of the themes highlighted by the modernity–post-modernity debate and themes familiar to Christianity. The purpose of this exercise is not to reduce or subordinate one set of ideas to another, which would only serve the purpose of denying very real differences, but, rather, to open up a discussion that allows for the possibility of each side taking the other seriously and engaging in a search for some common ground. I want to suggest that we may have some things to learn from each other.

Church as dialogical community

We need, perhaps, to remind ourselves of the context in which we are now working, both as described by the theoreticians of post-modernity and those of us who have been practitioners at a local level. The key term is 'fragmentation', as earlier applied to communities, social relationships, patterns of belief and ethical and political practice. So, for instance, national churches can no longer claim to be at the heart of matters and the local church cannot be seen as the hub of community life. In a pluralist culture, both are merely two fragments among many and there is no longer one tradition or set of practices that provides the foundation or cement for our common life.

Society, then, is faced with a very difficult problem. How do we learn to live together in a way that both acknowledges and respects significant differences and yet provides enough common ground for peaceful co-operation and coexistence? We are aware of two extreme alternatives. On the one hand, each group, tradition or fragment could choose to remain aloof from the rest and pursue its own beliefs and practices regardless of the consequences for other groups. 'Society' would then become a battleground between competing factions and the role of government would be that of a neutral arbiter, maintaining the boundaries and trying to limit the damage resulting from the inevitable conflicts. Such a scenario already has its parallel within moral and political philosophy where the search is on for a purely procedural system of ethics that agrees solely on the rules for fair play and makes no claims in terms of content (see, for instance, the ideas of John Rawls and Jürgen Habermas[1]). Whether such a position is viable or desirable is seriously open to question.[2]

At the other extreme, we can imagine a situation in which one group gains a monopoly of political and/or military power and succeeds in imposing its will on the rest at the expense of human liberty and life in general. We may well believe that we have seen such systems operating in the Communist world and developing nations, although recent events reveal the gaps between the rhetoric and the reality. However, whatever form it would take, this is a scenario that most of us would prefer to avoid.

Is there a middle way between these two extremes? If there is not, then prospects for the future become somewhat bleak. I want to ground this discussion by returning to the local example for a moment.

In Shropshire, the Church of England represents merely one fragment of local society and there are significant other groups that do not relate to it or remain on the margins. What should the local congregation be trying to work towards in this situation?

It could become an enclosed group, existing only for itself, pandering to the tastes of those who provide the financial support. It could go out into the wider community and attempt to convert the other groups, denying differences and trying to produce a type of religious clone. Neither of these scenarios is satisfactory, although both can be encountered regularly in local churches.

A third way would be to acknowledge one's position as a fragment, but, at the same time, recognize that the greatest need is to bring the various fragments together, not for open conflict or conversion, but for conversation. Such an approach would have to be carefully qualified. It would not entail the claim that the church was a uniquely privileged fragment, fulfilling a role that no other could play. Neither could it claim a structure that would hold all the other fragments together. The role is definitely not a foundational one and neither could the local congregation claim to be a neutral arbiter, refereeing the ensuing discussion from a distanced or objective standpoint. It could only work if there was first an open acknowledgement of vested interests and beliefs and then a willingness to let go of them sufficiently to allow others into the conversation.

One can see that this differs from the procedural approach in that it owns the substantive and partial views held by church members (as by all others). Such a vision is certainly difficult to pursue, but that it is possible to move towards it is witnessed by the work of the Local History Group, described in the last chapter.

What resources might the local church have to offer in this setting? First, a place to meet, and, second, an excuse for meeting. We should not underestimate the straightforward significance of possessing property that is normally used for public purposes, nor that of being able to bring people together, not just for worship, but for discussion.[3] Perhaps the greatest advantage that the church possesses is that it can legitimately initiate discussion of any issue at a moral or spiritual level. I suggest that this may be crucial. Part of the problem in contemporary society is that what might be termed moral issues, for instance, humanity's relationships with the natural world or family life, tend to be reduced to a functional or economic level because of the predominantly instrumental values of an industrial, capitalistic society.[4] Judgements and decisions are made largely on the basis of how much financial benefit or sacrifice are involved or on how effectively actions will meet the working requirements of the economy. One way to resist this is to carve out spaces and opportunities for issues to be discussed in such a way that the moral dimension is included. Local churches already have these, if they choose to use them this way.

As has been described elsewhere,[5] the trap that the church so often falls into is that of feeling obliged to make pronouncements on every issue from a distinctive, Christian perspective. The effect of this is often to limit the potential for allowing a wider discussion in which any Christian viewpoint is just one of many. The end result is, I believe, a missed opportunity to offer an even more valuable service to contemporary society—that of creating space for the debates that must take place if the two extreme scenarios are to be avoided.

In the discussion surrounding modernity–post-modernity, such an option has been described by Richard J. Bernstein as the search for a dialogical community.[6] Among other things, this presupposes a commitment by all groups to engage in an open discussion of differences, and an attempt to identify and avoid all the distortions that so often impinge on human communication as the result of the uneven distribution of power within society. In other words, as was noted earlier, everybody should be able to name their reality and have it acknowledged and respected within a wider forum. In practice, it is never fully possible to counteract the power-related distortions that prevent this vision being realized. However, the value of the idea of a dialogical community is that it offers something positive to work towards.

It seems to me that this is a vision that Christians might also share and to which we could make a practical contribution. We have, after all, the idea of respect for one another enshrined in the notion of love of neighbour. One contemporary implementation of this could be the willingness to engage in the open discussion required by the dialogical community. The other Christian contribution would be the legitimizing process of dealing with the four levels of human functioning described in the third mediating framework. That is, we recognize that human beings do not work exclusively, or even largely, at a rational–intellectual level, but at the levels of the practical and transpersonal consciousness, and the unconscious, too. One of the weaknesses of the philosophical descriptions of the dialogical community is that they rely too heavily on a critical consciousness.

It is important to consider under what conditions the vision could be realized, however inadequately. One significant factor would be a sense of self-confidence and self-worth for the individuals and groups involved. This is where local community projects can be so important in encouraging both these qualities in people at the margins of society. However, even more crucially, there will be a need for a high degree of trust: trust that others will be prepared to respect one's position and not exploit information revealed in the open discussion for their own benefit. This sounds almost impossibly idealistic as, even with the very best of intentions and highest of motives, human beings are rarely capable of this degree of open-handedness.

This, though, raises a serious doubt about the whole project if the necessary level of trust is impossible to guarantee within human relationships as normally experienced. It is not enough to say, as Habermas does, that there are, within language itself, criteria for assessing open and trustworthy communication.[7] What he cannot explain is why anybody should be prepared to enter into this sort of risky project when most of our experiences suggest that we would be naive and foolish to do so. Can there be any final guarantee or guarantor of this trust?

It would be very tempting at this juncture to leap into the breech with stock Christian answers. For instance, the ideal of love of neighbour becomes the motivation behind our respect for the other person, or God becomes the third person in the conversation, mediating, overseeing that there is fair play, and guaranteeing ultimate trust. Perhaps, from within the Christian tradition, these are the things we ought to be saying. The problem is that of using such explicit Christian language in a setting that requires a more radical letting go of established positions. Provided that we are aware of this and sensitive to the discourses and beliefs of others, it becomes appropriate that we think of the dialogical community in these terms for ourselves. This is where we can begin to see parallels with the discourse of Christian spirituality. The letting go required can only be enabled by a growth in self-worth, and, then, a trust in one beyond ourselves who will remain trustworthy despite all human capriciousness and inconsistency. God becomes the hope and the guarantor of human communication and can inspire us to continue working towards the ideal of such a community, even though the weight of evidence is against it.

A basis for critique

Critique in the name of what? This question poses one of the key dilemmas for the philosophers of post-modernity. It appears to be the case that those who are most acutely conscious of the challenges facing a pluralist and fragmented culture deny more than they affirm. For instance, they point out the breakdown of grand narratives, the impossibility of achieving final or definitive interpretations of any text and the hidden contradictions and dangers within all discourses.[8] However, somewhere in this process of deconstruction and critique one would imagine that there needed to be something positive. After all, why criticize a particular way of doing things or of looking at the world unless one has a better alternative to offer?

It is at this point that post-modernists tend to be at their weakest. There is often very little clear exposition of what the *future* should look like, only resolute descriptions of the inadequacies of the *present*. Once again, this is an area in which Christianity might be tempted to intervene with stock answers. However, is not this the value of having symbols like the kingdom of God, so that we have something positive to work towards? In a way this is true, but it disguises the fact that the symbol cannot be pinned down to any specific content. It is more like a regulative ideal, a counter-factual, as is the notion of a dialogical community. We can see what it is we should be aiming for in general terms, but we are aware that we are never going to reach it, that whatever stage we have reached, the journey is not yet over. So, what is significant about the symbol is not any substantive content that we might attribute to it, but the function that it plays within the life of the Christian community.

It feels, then, as though post-modernists are in a similar position to ourselves. The major difference is that they are fully aware that there are any number of such regulative ideals at work within different discourses: for Zen it is Sartori, for a Buddhist Nirvana, for a Marxist the classless society, for a Christian the kingdom of God, for a Habermasian the ideal communication community; and so on.[9] This is not to say that they all really mean the same thing—far from it— but they *can* perform a similar function.

The problems begin, inevitably, when attempts are made to attribute more substantive content to regulative ideals. For instance, for the post-modernist there is the deeply disturbing question of the viability of establishing a rational basis for the critique of society when it is the distortions in human reason that dominate our interpretation of that society. Is reason still to be trusted? If not, how can we formulate the meaning of the good life or portray the shape of a better world? For the Christian, there is the struggle to work towards the kingdom of God, but, all the time, there is also the awareness that our personalities and relationships are flawed, so the ideal is forever just beyond our grasp.

We appear to be faced again with two extreme possibilities: either we place our trust unquestioningly in these ideas and in the human capacity to achieve them, or we recognize their ultimate unrealizability and give up in despair.

The way forward is to do neither of these, but, instead, to hold on to the hope of a better future while simultaneously retaining a realistic perspective on what can be achieved. In all of our local projects it would have been very easy to give up hope, but, at other times, we were perhaps misguidedly optimistic about what we had achieved. The truth usually lay somewhere in between. Perhaps very little had changed, but even that amount of change had to be worthwhile, and provide the stimulus and confidence for further action. Christians and post-modernists, therefore, seem to be working according to the same system. The point of the description that now follows is to build possible bridges between the two to assist in the process of relating Christianity to the cultured despisers of religion.

To turn for a moment to the discussers of post-modernity. On the one hand we encounter thinkers such as Habermas who wish to retain some of the Enlightenment hope in human reason by portraying its contemporary manifestations as a distortion. Thus, reason now largely employed within industrial culture as a means of calculating either what best serves self-interest or the needs of the economy needs to be replaced by communicative reason, which assumes intersubjectivity and the priority of human interaction. Within this, reason serves the purpose of working against distortions in human communication, facilitating the open discussions of the dialogical community.[10]

On the other hand, we read in the works of Derrida and Foucault of the dangers and ambiguities of such hopes in this reformulated reason. Ideas that advocate authentic dialogue, renewed community and communicative rationality can themselves become 'suffocating straightjackets' and 'enslaving conceptions'.[11] Communication in an administered world becomes little more than the technological exchange of information put to the service of the profit motive. Habermas glosses over the problem of how there can be authentic dialogue unless there is at least some sharing of values, commitments, and even feelings. He cannot explain why anybody should engage in communicative reason and the problem is that any potential answers—love of neighbour or the struggle of the proletariat—are always in danger of being distorted. Within the very language used by the various traditions lie the seeds of the universal claims and metaphysical views that feed the power-plays we claim to resist.[12] So, we have the ideals of reformulated community, but the constant risks of imposing a false commonality—of reducing others to pale reflections of ourselves.

Then, there are the spokespersons of the marginalized groups, always conscious of their differences but in danger of emphasizing them to the point where contact with others becomes an impossibility. There are both sameness and radical alterity, both symmetry and asymmetry, identity and difference in our relationships with others. The task is to do justice to and respect this 'both/and' structure.[13]

Within a Christian discourse, we have ways of reflecting similar tensions and paradoxes: we are both sinners and saved, unacceptable and yet accepted;[14] we are citizens of heaven and still fully engaged in this world; we are created to be at one in our relationships and all of them contain elements of brokenness and inadequacy. The harmony, community and wholeness sought by Habermas are familiar themes, but so, too, are the ambiguities, contradictions and discontinuities described by a Derrida or Foucault. Once again, this is not to say one set of ideas is the same as the other, but merely to point out some significant parallels. Perhaps Christianity and post-modernity are not so far apart after all.

The private and the public

One of the consequences of the growing predominance of an instrumental reason has been the divorce of public and political matters from the discourses on morality and values. The latter are now concerns for the individual only, neither to be imposed on others, nor become the basis for any form of collective decision making. Values are now no longer so much part of belonging to a tradition, but, rather, another area in which consumer choice can be exercised. We choose which life-style options to explore and personal morality becomes subject to trial and experiment.[15]

While some post-modern thinkers, such as Richard Rorty,[16] fully advocate this approach as the only viable option for a liberal society, in the works of Habermas, Foucault and Derrida we can detect strong echoes of a demand to cross the barrier between private and public. Habermas is the most overtly political of the three, but Derrida expresses this dimension in his concern for marginalized groups and Foucault in his analyses of power.[17] What, perhaps, each is searching for, in a different way, is a rehumanizing of political life. The truth, of course, is that politics is always value-laden and the people with most to gain from concealing or denying this are those whose values are embedded in current political practice. It is up to the losers in the system to draw this out.

In this sense, it is the new social movements that are the grass-roots manifestation of this process (for a fuller discussion of these, see Chapter 7). Concern for the environment, for greater control over our own bodies, for the rights of minority groups, and so on, are attempts to feed back into the political agenda issues that have become restricted to the level of personal morality.[18] The weakness of these movements is that, because they are largely focused on single issues, the major political parties can always divide and conquer. They lack a single or commonly-held argument by means of which they could engage existing political power blocs. In order to gain greater access to these, new social movements have to risk compromising their political principles. They learn to play the system and, thereby, become implicated in its distortions and abuses. It is important for Christians who become involved in this form of collective action to be aware of these dangers.[19]

It is clear that recent calls for an integrated spirituality are also attempts to cross the divide between the private and the public.[20] In terms of my own third mediating framework, this would be represented by the suggestion that an authentic spirituality would address social and political as well as personal issues. Once more, it would seem that we can identify parallel concerns between a strand of contemporary Christianity and some post-modern thinkers and activists.

The local and the universal

A practical implication of suspecting all universal claims, now registered by such thinkers as Derrida and Foucault, is that we are left with limited options for the starting point for any critique. Foucault, for instance, suggests that the most we can hope for are localized critiques of power. In his efforts to avoid all global terms, he redirects our attention to what is local, specific, and historically contingent. In so far as critique is aimed at opening up new possibilities for thinking, and acting on and locating where change is possible and desirable, it must be appropriated by those who have been marginalized. Indeed, a major aim of Foucault's work is to show how different discourses have been used to exclude, marginalize and limit sections of humanity.[21]

We need to acknowledge the value of this work and recognize its potential affinity with a local approach to theology. As I suggested earlier, theology for those on the margins needs to have a different format to the traditional one now taught at universities and training institutions. However, it also returns us to the dilemma of how to communicate either a theology or a political critique of a local nature to a wider constituency. If either become so specific and localized as to resist any generalization, then a vital part of the task is rendered impossible.

As with the new social movements, local theologies could easily fall prey to the limitations of being single-issue groups, unable to mobilize effectively against broader political power structures, and so fail to gain wider credibility. This is where Habermas' work is so instructive, because he has attempted to provide procedural common ground that could hold together the different strands of political protest.[22] I would say that this parallels my own attempts to construct mediating frameworks that provide some way of moving from the local to the more general.

As noted earlier, however, the problem with what Habermas suggests is that it tries to exclude all substantive moral content. In fact, it is not possible to do this (even Habermas covertly espouses particular values in his system), nor do I believe that it is appropriate to do this. If part of the task is to acknowledge and respect differences, then these need to be named within the process (hence the mention made earlier of the importance of laying the cards on the table at the very beginning of any open discussion). Once more, though, we have identified a common theme with local theology—a struggle to work out how to relate the local to the wider in an environment where universal claims are no longer acceptable.

Letting go: detachment and engagement

As previously, the scenario that faces us is one of working out how to live within an apparently irreconcilable tension. In order to acknowledge the full humanity of the other person or group, one has to be secure enough to recognize differences and not feel threatened by them. This requires a willingness to let go of, or at least to see in a wider perspective, one's feelings and beliefs. On the other hand, there is always the danger, if one goes too far in this direction, of submerging one's own differences beneath the encounter with the other. Somewhere in this there has to be a balance, a reciprocity that respects the integrity of all parties.

In a moment I will draw on resources from Christian spirituality that may further illuminate this tension. However, it is important to first add a note of caution. It will not always be the case that differences should be respected merely because they *are* differences. Apartheid, for instance, may be a different political structure to our own but it is not appropriate to honour it in this way. It is clear, therefore, that an uncritical celebration of plurality, differences and otherness harbours its own dangers. What is too frequently obscured if we follow thinkers like Derrida all the way is the need to make critical determinations and judgements. We can end up with a form of tribalism in which differences and otherness are reified and where there is a failure to seek out commonalities and similarities.

This is why we need the counterbalance of thinkers such as Habermas, who wants to retain the notion of a critique based on universal validity claims. If we abandon the exercise of discrimination, then anything goes and the result is either total anarchy, or a consensus imposed by force. We have to be able to say that there are both similarities *and* differences; both potential reconciliation *and* the possibility of ruptures and disintegration. This is the dichotomy of life.

How, then, can we account for critique if it is no longer acceptable to establish any definitive or universal ground rules for its operation? We can agree with Foucault that all critique is local and specific, but also acknowledge that this does not excuse us from the task of defending and explaining to others where we stand and why. Hence, our mediating frameworks. We have to be clear that we engage in critique as second-person participants and not as third-person neutral observers. So, inevitably, the standpoints that we adopt are tentative, fallible, and provisional. We live and move in the space between doubt and conviction.

Perhaps one of the clearest parallels we can find in Christian spirituality is the work of Meister Eckhart.[23] The process of the transformation of the self on the path to mystical or transpersonal awareness presupposes a willingness to let go. First, one must learn to let go of things as possessions, because we need to learn that we do not have to define who we *are* by what we possess. If we can do this, then the things are free to be themselves and do not have to exist only as they are for us. Once we have learned this, we begin to realize that the same is true in our relationships with other people. They do not exist for *our* benefit, to meet *our* individual needs and requirements, as resources to be used, but rather in their *own* right. This can only happen to the extent that we are genuinely secure within ourselves. Then we will know that we can be ourselves without being dependent on others. Letting others be themselves as they are, not as they are for us, releases all of us to discover a greater depth of relationship founded on trust.

Does this not bear at least some resemblance to Derrida's concerns for otherness and difference? Perhaps some of the Christian mystics have offered us glimpses of the conditions in which respect for the other can become a reality. The danger with this, as with Derrida's ideas, is that if there is *only* detachment and disengagement, a letting go and withdrawing from what is distinctive about oneself or one's group, then the other and otherness take over. We become empty vessels into which other people pour their needs and desires. This is a highly dangerous strategy, both personally and politically.

What is being advocated here only makes sense if it can become the basis for a more radical engagement with others and the world. Losing oneself should not mean abandoning oneself to others, but discovering a better way of being together. We can become engaged in the world in a different way: less aggressive, less determined to make others like ourselves, less dependent on external roles or material success, and take ourselves less seriously. This will not be because nothing matters or is really important to us, but because they matter in a different way. We are here on this planet together, no more or less important than anything or anybody else.

If this is right, then there is a dialectic between detachment and engagement, between objective or communicative rationality and a passionate involvement. Both are necessary, but neither of them will stand alone. Periods of withdrawal are as important as times of fulfilling activity. There is nothing new in this, although we perhaps need to rediscover it in our own age and for ourselves.

Conclusion

Where does this leave us in our conversations with other parts of ourselves and with the cultured despisers of religion? I suggest that there is much of value for all parties to discover in a teasing out of both new ideas and established traditions. The new may not be so new after all and some of the old may be more contemporary than we thought. The practical implications could be immense, particularly for a post-modern Christianity that aims to hold together the personal and the political, the rational and the emotional. As has been suggested elsewhere, this may be a key to the moral dilemmas now facing us, especially our relationships with the natural world.[24] Living in a dichotomy may be the only safe place to be.

Notes

1 John Rawls, *A Theory of Justice*. Oxford University Press 1972. Jürgen Habermas, *Communication and the Evolution of Society*. Heinemann Educational 1979.
2 Agnes Heller, *Beyond Justice* (Basil Blackwell 1987), pp. 232–44.
3 Ian Ball, Margaret Goodall, Clare Palmer, John Reader, eds, *The Earth Beneath* (SPCK 1992), Chapter 7.
4 Jürgen Habermas, *The Theory of Communicative Action*,Vol. 2. Boston, Beacon Press, 1987.
5 Ball, Goodall, Palmer and Reader.
6 Richard J. Bernstein, *Beyond Objectivism and Relativism* (Basil Blackwell 1983), Part 4.
7 Habermas, *Communication and the Evolution of Society* p. 2ff.
8 Michel Foucault, *The History of Sexuality*, Vol. 1. Penguin 1990.
9 John Hick, *An Interpretation of Religion* (Macmillan 1989), Chapter 3.
10 Bernstein, *Beyond Objectivism*.

11 Richard J. Bernstein, *The New Constellation* (Polity Press 1991), p. 51.
12 Christopher Norris, *Derrida* (Fontana 1987), p. 109.
13 Bernstein, *New Constellation*, p. 70.
14 Paul Tillich, *The Shaking of the Foundations* (Penguin 1962), p. 163.
15 Anthony Giddens, *Modernity and Self-identity* (Polity Press 1991), Chapter 3.
16 Richard Rorty, *Contingency, Irony and Solidarity*. Cambridge University Press 1989.
17 Bernstein, *New Constellation*, Chapter 6.
18 Alberto Melucci, *Nomads of the Present* (Hutchinson Radius 1989), Chapter 5.
19 Ball, Goodall, Palmer and Reader, Chapter 2.
20 Donal Dorr, *Integral Spirituality*. Dublin, Gill & Macmillan, 1990.
21 Bernstein, *New Constellation*, Chapter 5.
22 Habermas, *Theory of Communicative Action*.
23 Robert K. C. Forman, *Meister Eckhart: Mystic as Theologian*. Element Books 1991.
24 Ball, Goodall, Palmer and Reader, Chapter 5.

5

Friends of Hopesay Meadow
Environmental Project

An issue for the faith community

The major requirement of the local faith community as identified through the local theology project was to create an environment within which people could begin to express more openly and confidently the various dimensions of their religious experience. In order to facilitate this process, I suggested a mediating framework that pointed to four different levels at which human beings function: the unconscious, practical consciousness, critical consciousness, and transpersonal consciousness. We have already seen in earlier chapters how much of the work currently underway, both with those on the margins of society and with the cultured despisers of religion, involves a process of consciousness-raising. This can be described as a shift from the everyday routine operation of the practical consciousness to the more questioning and reflective approach associated with the critical consciousness.

Within church groups a similar process is at work through lay training and continued ministerial education. Christians are encouraged to stand back from their direct involvement and use methods of analysis to consider critically both their actions and the thinking behind them. This was one cf the functions that the Local History Group played for the Christians who were part of it. However, the project that I am now going to describe raised a somewhat different dimension.

99

There is no doubt that the question of humanity's relationship with the natural world has become a contemporary focus for a discussion about how our feelings, intuitions and creativity should contribute to the life of the faith community. In terms of the mediating framework, we are dealing with levels one and four—the unconscious or at least pre-rational responses to nature that lie behind much of the environmental debate and their possible link to the search for oneness with both creation and creator that characterize significant strands of Christian mysticism and spirituality (a more detailed discussion of this takes place in Chapter 6). The aim of this present chapter is to show how these issues arose from the local, practical engagement with environmental issues.

Why the environment?

It is not easy to identify one specific conversation or event with the start of this project. However, in retrospect, it is possible to point to a number of strands or ideas that eventually came together. First, there was the discussion of environmental issues during the initial meeting of the Local History Group, as reported earlier. However, even that may be traced further back to the exhibition of parish maps held at the Community College. Second, there was a particular local occurrence that highlighted the issue for a number of us. This was a violent, summer thunderstorm, during which very heavy rain fell on the steep hillside just behind the village. The fields had just been prepared for the sowing of oil seed rape, and the water picked up much of the loosened top soil with the chemicals in it and swept a torrent of mud down on to the village. Damage was done, but, fortunately, nobody was hurt. There were complaints that the local estate had cultivated fields that, in previous times, would have been left for pasture, and removed hedges that might have held back the worst of the mud. Suddenly, the subject of the environment was a live issue because the evidence of intensive farming was on peoples' well-kept lawns and on the odd living-room carpet.

It seems that it is necessary for there to be an event where people's interests and safety are directly at stake in order to arouse a concern for the environment. However, this disaster was like the final, catalytic event in a consciousness-raising process that had already started. There was a growing concern, even within the farming community. Smaller farmers, in particular, would talk in apologetic terms about the necessity of using chemicals. Farm workers' wives were beginning to express anxiety about the illnesses their children were contracting and linking these to the chemicals their husbands were told to spray on to the fields. At the County Council election, the Tory candidate, who was used to being returned unopposed, beat a Green candidate by only sixty-seven votes. Each of these elements, trivial, perhaps, in themselves, contributed to an increasing sense of concern about our treatment of the environment.

There was a further dimension to this concern that emerged through the Local History Group. The environment was one of the issues that divided locals and newcomers. The latter had a habit of importing trendy ideas about organic farming and healthier life-styles, and talking about them as if the farming community did not know anything and should abandon less ecologically sound methods and go Green. The farming community was quick to point out that they were the ones who had to make a living from the land and knew what was and was not possible. There is also the claim that country people have always been the best conservationists anyway and that sports like fox hunting preserve habitats that otherwise would be lost. The environment was a divisive issue.

When the Local History Group began, there was a feeling that what was missing was a forum in which the two sides could come together and conduct a reasoned discussion. People had felt as though there were two separate camps shouting at each other from distant hilltops when what was needed was a willingness to come down into the valley and listen to the various points of view. All existing local groups were partisan and could not provide neutral ground. The concern underlying this was still the nature of community life. Was there a way in which the different fragments could be drawn together?

It became clear, however, that such a hope was somewhat idealistic. Each side invariably felt too threatened by the other to engage in open dialogue. Perhaps what was needed was a practical focus for the discussion that could draw people into the wider debate in a less threatening manner. This was certainly one motive for setting up a local environmental project. Another was to continue the process of consciousness-raising, particularly within church circles. There were those who believed that, as Christians, we should have a contribution to make to the environmental debate and that a project would stir people into responding, whether positively or negatively. A third motivation was to begin to build bridges to those outside the established church who were both concerned with the environment and interested in spiritual matters. Finally, this would be another community project that could provide all the benefits of learning new skills and building confidence that others were learning from the play scheme.

The project

Setting this up proved to be an education in its own right, and it is too difficult to recount all the subtle nuances of the story here, but I will offer an outline because I believe it will shed light on some key questions for a local theology and be of benefit to others with similar ideas.

The scheme began to form in the minds of four members of the Local History Group when we learned that one of the churches owned some land. Of course, it was not as simple as that—it never is. The Vicar and church wardens held in trust, for the benefit of the local primary school children, a small piece of land on a hill overlooking the church, most of which was owned by the National Trust. The PCC owned another piece of land directly adjacent to the existing churchyard that had been purchased in the days when an extension had seemed a likely necessity.

Nothing had been said openly in the PCC about either piece of land until the question arose about the future of the primary school. If it were to close, what were the trustees to do? Both lots were lying fallow and had been more or less forgotten until now. Once we realized that this land was possibly available, those of us on the PCC who were part of the Local History Group saw the possibilities. We were beginning to learn the lessons of setting up the play scheme: first, spot the openings. The second lesson was, find an outside person who has the skills and knowledge to help you set up the project.

We again contacted the Rural Officer at the Community Council. She said that this was not within her remit, exactly, but put us in touch with an officer of the Shropshire Wildlife Trust. Before long, he arrived to carry out a site visit with us and gave us the benefit of his advice. He recommended that we did not pursue any plans to turn the plot on the hillside into an environmental area, but concentrate our energies, instead, on the land next to the churchyard, which seemed a much more viable proposition. He offered to draw up a management plan for us and become part of a local project should we succeed in setting it up. The seeds had been sown, or at least, they would be if we could get enough support.

The next step was to sell the idea to the PCC. Given the history of power struggles that had already emerged from listening to the local stories, plus the tensions between locals and newcomers that cut through all activities in the area, we could hardly expect to be in for an easy ride. The challenge would be to present the proposal in such a way that the normal blocking arguments would be rendered useless. If this sounds like Barchester writ small, this is probably because there is some truth in such a description.

It was some months after the original site meeting that the proposal was first mentioned at a PCC meeting. We had invited the newly appointed Agricultural Chaplain to the Diocese along to the meeting, partly to give the scheme legitimacy from outside, and in the hope that the potential opposition would hold its fire with an outsider present. Eyebrows were raised in certain quarters when the scheme was presented, but nothing was said openly. The normal tactic in the past had been to snipe at ideas and undermine plans once public meetings were over, but we had made it clear that both the discussion and decision process would take place in open meetings. There is a fascinating lesson to be learned from this about the exercising of power. As we had discovered at the time of the debate within the Parish Council on the housing survey, the local establishment did not like, and were not very good at, open confrontation, largely because they had never needed to use this tactic; they were used to winning their battles behind the scenes.

It soon became clear that the PCC would not agree to sponsor an environmental project itself. However, we found a way round this by setting up a separate committee with its own constitution that would still be accountable to the PCC. This, too, became quite complicated though, not to say farcical, with drafts of the constitution going backwards and forwards between the various key people before it was finally accepted by the PCC. The objective in this was clearly to make the process as difficult as possible in the hope that the scheme would be abandoned as its proponents ran out of enthusiasm and energy. Having realized that the battle would be lost in open forum, the opposition opted for delaying tactics. Fortunately, we had received valuable briefing on how to draw up constitutions for community organizations from the Community Council, so we knew what we were doing and just had to be determined.

I remember thinking that we had finally won when the only argument that could be put forward against the project was that the land might one day be needed for a car park for the church. As cars did not have access to this piece of land and there was a more likely need for extra graveyard space that tarmacing the land would preclude, but turning it into an environmental area would not, I felt that such an argument really was a last resort. It was and the battle was over.

On one level, none of this has anything to do with the environmental issue, it is all about power. However, given the social structure of the area, it was impossible to establish new schemes through the church without facing this dimension. In such a structure, any change is resisted as a matter of principle because it threatens to disturb the norm. The *content* of the change is irrelevant, which is why it is so difficult to establish a serious, rational discussion of the real issues. Newcomers are a challenge and a threat whatever they happen to suggest. They either have to be absorbed into the existing structures, or left firmly on the outside where they can do little real damage. Even then the ideas of newcomers can have no real impact on lower-class local people, who are still subject to the same power structure.

It must be recognized that some rural churches are riddled with these attitudes and so more radical approaches to ministry are going to be faced with considerable opposition. A local theology in this context will be forced to confront questions of injustice and power in a very personal way. In an urban setting, the same questions arise, but, more often, this happens in dealings with impersonal bodies and organizations, which can make them more difficult to confront. The other difference is that, in rural areas, those on the other side in the struggle are more likely to be members of local congregations and influential financial supporters of the church.

The environmental issue highlighted an ambiguity that we discussed in the original meeting of the Local History Group. On the surface, going Green always sounds like an unimpeachable ideal, but, in a capitalistic political structure, one must always ask who is benefitting from any changes in policy. The ecological idealists would say that this is to put human interests above the good of the natural world, and this is true, but how can those who may have to suffer as a result of the introduction of environmentally sound policies be expected to support such action? It will still be those in the higher reaches of the social and political structures who will reap the benefits, as in most other new commercial enterprises. If Christians are to tackle the environmental question, they must not make the mistake of doing so in isolation, but, instead, in the wider context of social justice. The local experience made this quite clear.

Wider questions

It is five years since the project was first conceived, and so now is an appropriate time to carry out an interim assessment of how successful it has been. On the surface, it has been *highly* successful. The original management plan has been implemented and the meadow is open for the public to enjoy as an amenity area, and an example others can use to learn from. It has received financial support from a number of agencies, including the Countryside Commission, the Royal Society for Nature Conservation, Shell UK, UK 2000, and Shropshire County Council. The project was put on to a shortlist of seven such enterprises for a national award from Shell. So, the meadow, as it was envisaged by the group that set it up, is now in existence and has been given quite a lot of publicity.

All this is very encouraging. However, to what extent has it achieved some of the other objectives that were outlined at the start of the project? It could not be claimed that it has provided a focus for more open discussion of environmental issues, for example, as the battle lines between environmentalists and the local farming community remain firmly in place. As far as local farmers are concerned, the whole project is a waste of time and another example of trendy newcomers trying to tell everyone else how to live. It may be that this will change in time. Such changes of attitude take a long time, and the fact that the meadow is there stands as a symbol and a reminder to others that another approach to the natural world is possible, even if they do not agree with it.

The consciousness-raising achieved within the church is difficult to measure. The project has drawn new members from the community rather than from the local congregation, and that, in itself, is a good thing. Some original church members already involved in Green issues are still part of the project, and are the essential link between the two groups. The connection with Shropshire Wildlife Trust has created opportunities for its officers to speak to other local groups, including the Women's Institute, and this represents a step forward. Within the wider church, this has to be seen as a small part of a growing movement to get local churches to consider carefully how they use their land, particularly churchyards, and there is a national project based at the Arthur Rank Centre at Stoneleigh that is at the centre of this. I suspect that those who get involved are already sympathetic to Green issues, but it does give them the chance to raise the necessary questions at a local level that they would not otherwise be able to do in such a positive way.

As a community project, the meadow has probably been slightly less successful than the play scheme, in that it has failed to draw in other sections of the local population, although there are a few exceptions. This may have something to do with the nature of the project itself—it appeals only to a narrow interest group, whereas the play scheme had a broader appeal. It may also reflect the more fragmented character of this particular community, within which it is difficult in any case to generate much community spirit. Even the plan to build a new village hall split the community, although that project did gain wider support than the meadow.

Another factor was the closure of the primary school,

which was initially deeply involved with the meadow project. Children came to it to carry out natural history projects and helped to stock the pond that was constructed, as well as doing some of the planting. The loss of the school was a serious blow to both the meadow and the wider community.

On the other hand, those who did give their time and energy learned a considerable amount. First, the pleasures of being outdoors and working with a group of people with whom they shared a common aim. The Saturday-morning working parties were worth holding in their own right as they did draw people closer together. There was also a sense in which working outdoors increased our awareness of nature and our own role within it, developing an understanding of its inherent value. Those who dealt with the financial side of the project, notably the fundraising, learned much about current attitudes towards Green issues and how to play the funding system. At times we wondered about the morality of making such sums available for schemes like ours when other equally worthy projects could not attract any funds. There is, of course, also a deep irony when you examine the environmental track records of some of the organizations that provide funding. To what extent is this just conscience money? On the other hand, they are an important source of finance. This is how ideas borne out of a reaction against the capitalist system are drawn back into its clutches.

What involvement with the scheme did do for some of its members was to give them contacts with other sections of the environmental movement. Here we can clearly see the poppy seeds being scattered in varying directions and generating new growth. To offer an example. One of the group attended a meeting in London set up by an agency working closely with the then World Wildlife Fund (WWF), now the Worldwide Fund for Nature (WFN). An interest had been expressed in the Creation Harvest organized by WWF at Winchester Cathedral and there were plans to develop such services at other venues. As a result of this meeting, the man at the centre of these plans came down to Shropshire to the Community College to see if there might be any local involvement. A clergy colleague, who was experienced in leading pilgrimages, was then asked by WWF to organize one of four national pilgrimages to the Creation Festival held at Canterbury Cathedral in 1989. A number of young people from the High School were also involved in this.

We had some reservations about the whole operation. While we recognized the role of WWF in raising awareness of environmental issues, we had doubts about the way in which they used local material. It seemed to us as though their main purpose was to gather and even, if necessary, to doctor, material that then became a convenient part of their publicity machine. Perhaps this is an inevitable consequence of having to use the mass media, which are more often concerned with what will produce a good short documentary piece than with providing an accurate picture of the local perspective. Such an approach is not consistent with a local theology, which is concerned to give a voice to local people. This does not happen when accounts are appropriated by outsiders. This, again, raises interesting questions about the environmental movement as it can end up playing the same games as its opponents.

A further dimension to this is more explicitly theological. Behind this whole debate lie questions of how we find appropriate language to describe humanity's relationship to the natural world. Much theological material concentrates on this issue and attempts to revive elements of the Christian tradition that appear to be environmentally friendly, such as the notion of stewardship. Our local discussions revealed an unease about this approach. For one thing, the model of a steward suggested to us a farm manager, hardly the most suitable way of describing a more sympathetic attitude towards nature, with all due respect to farm managers. Another problem was that such attempts to redefine familiar Christian terminology did not have much impact on those living locally who were already deeply committed to the Green cause, but suspicious of the established churches because of their bad track record on other issues. If part of what we wanted to do was to build bridges to these sections of the community, then we had to start taking their ideas and criticisms of the church more seriously. Something more radical was called for.

Being engaged in a grass roots project was, at least, a good way of showing others that this was not just talk, but led to practical action and an attempt to manage church land more responsibly. Being part of a national event on the environment also raised the profile of this involvement locally. However, what was missing was a forum for more detailed discussions about how Christians should be responding to the environmental debate in wider terms. Having followed up a number of different contacts, we set up an informal, twenty-four-hour conference in the locality to try to further this discussion. The common ground that emerged was, on the one hand, an unease about current theological approaches that seemed to domesticate the debate, and, on the other, an equal dissatisfaction with the naively romantic and optimistic theorizing of many within the Green movement. Was there not another way?

This first conference led to a second. The aim of this was to produce some substantial, written response to such questions. This resulted in a book, contributions to which came from most of those involved in the conference. It is obviously not appropriate to repeat the arguments presented in the book here, but it is worth saying that one of its major aims was to shift the level of debate and to get the church to take more seriously some of the deeper questions raised by the environmental issue, in particular that surrounding the uncertainty over human identity. Whatever the success of the project, it would probably not have happened at all without the practical, local involvement that had occurred at Hopesay Meadow. It was through this that such deeper questions began to emerge, and it may be that any answers that we provided will feed back into future projects.

One final thought. It is vital to set such schemes in a wider political context. The issues will be taken up in more detail in the next chapter, but I would just like to say here that it became clear that any involvement with the environmental movement required a deeper understanding of the movement itself, its political potential, its capacity to provide a focus for human unease about contemporary society as well as its relationships to the Christian tradition—hence the conferences, and the book. It is all too easy for well-meaning Christians simply to jump on to the latest bandwagon without thinking any further. To do justice to both the contemporary issues *and* the tradition requires a more careful and considered response. Practical involvement at local level is probably the most appropriate way into the discussions, but they must not end there. A local theology must be prepared to follow the process through and engage with others asking similar questions.

6

A Critique of
Creation Spirituality

Introduction

One of the most significant and, indeed, popular attempts
from within the faith community to respond to environmental
issues is what is now being called 'Creation Spirituality'. As
in the previous two chapters, I will now use the insights
gained from local practical engagement with the issue to lead
into a discussion of wider concerns. I believe that it is possible to show both some of the inadequacies and some of the
strengths of this particular response.

What becomes clear from the experience of actually setting
up a local environmental project is that there is far more to
the process than simply a direct consideration of humanity's
relationship with the natural world. The themes that arose
from our work with the Friends of Hopesay Meadow included
power struggles within the community, ways of gaining
funding from commercial and charitable organizations, the
skills needed to establish a community project and the consciousness-raising that goes with that, and the necessity of
placing the local activity in its wider social and political
context.

Although one of the aims, probably, was to examine and
reflect on our relationship with creation, the project itself
would not have been possible without some consideration of
these other themes. It seems to me that this immediately
creates problems for a Creation Spirituality that moves directly

from the issue of our feelings for the natural world to a theological response. If we relate this to the third mediating framework, it suggests that there is a danger of shifting too easily and too rapidly from level one (that of the unconscious, the pre-rational or intuitive) to level four (that of mystical awareness, a sense of being at one with both creator and creation). How are we to *know* whether the feelings we have, for instance, as we walk across the South Shropshire hills are really a genuine route to our relationship with God or merely a flashback to our early experience of being undifferentiated from our own mother? This is far from being an academic issue as it may have serious political consequences. 'Back to nature' movements are not confined to the latter decades of the twentieth century, they were a part of the growth of National Socialism in Germany in the 1930s, for example.[1] To leave out of consideration wider social and political questions is, therefore, potentially dangerous.

There is a further concern here for Christianity itself. It is possible to interpret both some strands of Creation Spirituality and the New Age movement, with which it shares some common ground, as evidence of a 'pick and mix' approach to religion. In other words, with the breakdown of external religious authority now associated with post-modernity, people feel free to choose whatever suits them, from wherever they happen to find it, and create their own personal 'cocktail' of belief. Established religious institutions will, inevitably, fear that this will result in a state of anarchy in which it becomes impossible to hold the boundaries of any faith community. While such trends are undoubtedly in evidence, it seems to me inaccurate to suggest that we are faced simply with the two alternatives of either returning to submission to an external religious authority, or entering a free-for-all where each individual makes up their own religion. If there can be mediating frameworks, then there will be bases on which we can discuss our beliefs with others and in terms of which we can justify these beliefs. Belief does not have to become individualistic, anarchic, and arbitrary, even in modernity–post-modernity, provided that we can establish some criteria for conducting a public discussion.

What I suggest is that we use the third mediating framework as a means of exercising a critique of Creation Spirituality. In particular, given both the local experience and the wider political and religious considerations, we should require such an approach to show that it takes account of all four levels of human operation, and, especially, that it does not omit level three (that of the critical consciousness). What we will do now is examine two examples—one of Creation Spirituality, and one of a Green spirituality that does not make any claims to be specifically Christian—to see how they stand up to the criteria.

How, then, might we describe Creation Spirituality? As Matthew Fox is one of the main originators of this approach, I will use his definition.[2] He suggests that there are six key themes in Creation Spirituality. First, the goodness or the blessing of creation. This represents a wholly positive understanding of God's work of creation in contrast to more orthodox Christian views that underline the brokenness, or, in human terms, sin, that loom equally large in the whole picture. Second, the Earth itself is a blessing, including the human body. Once again, parts of the Christian tradition have appeared to denigrate all things to do with the body, and emphasized a disembodied spirituality. Fox wishes to redress the balance by going to the other extreme. Third, we should be working towards a cosmic awareness, or, consciousness—a psychology of microcosm and macrocosm, as he describes it, the sense that we are essentially interconnected, both with each other, and the natural world. Fourth, our relationship with God is most adequately expressed in a theology of panentheism. In other words, God is neither totally separate from the world, nor is he to be totally identified with it, as in pantheism. Panentheism has a good pedigree within Christianity, but the exact nature of the relationship between

God and the world still needs to be spelled out. Fifth, Fox draws to the foreground the notion of the 'motherhood' of God, and relates this to the idea that humanity's vocation is to be a co-creator of the cosmos: we share in God's work of creation in an intimate way. Finally, compassion is to be understood as interdependence and justice-making.

In order to ground these six themes in the Christian tradition, Fox cites such thinkers as Hildegaard of Bingen, Julian of Norwich and Meister Eckhart, as well as claiming that there are elements of this creation-centred approach in the Wisdom writings and those of the Old Testament prophets. Other manifestations occur in what is now called 'Celtic spirituality', and in the experience of women, who, like nature, have been exploited and oppressed.

Before we move on, it is worth pointing out that within Christianity there is a spectrum of views as to how God is related to the natural world, and, indeed, how humanity is related to it. At the one extreme lies the belief that God is a sort of mechanistic creator who first wound up the key and now has no more to do with his world. This is paralleled by the view that humans are totally set apart from nature, which thus becomes merely a resource to be used or exploited. At the other extreme lies pantheism, which sees God *as* the natural world—take the one away from the other and there will be nothing left over. Similarly, humans can also be totally identified with the rest of nature, not even consciousness or language separate us from it. Creation Spirituality stands somewhere between these two extremes, but with a heavy emphasis on closer relationships and interconnectedness. Such an emphasis is an understandable reaction to the mechanistic view often associated with the Enlightenment, and is now blamed for our destructive attitudes towards nature. It also has much in common with ideas emanating from some scientific circles, which advocate a holistic understanding of the universe.

What I want to do, briefly, is to examine Creation

Spirituality under three headings. First, to set it in an historical context. Second, to take two representative examples of a Green or Creation Spirituality—Matthew Fox and Charlene Spretnak—and engage in an evaluation of such views. Third, to offer some concluding comments.

An historical perspective

So far, three major responses to the environmental question have emerged from within the church. The first denies any real significance to the debate. The second recognizes this significance, but then wades in with stock Christian answers, not realizing that these may, in fact, be part of the problem. The third is Green all the way, using Christian ideas as a gloss for this position. Creation Spirituality, in its popular forms, is closest to the third response.

The argument that I now wish to pursue is that, in order to achieve a more balanced and considered response to these important questions, Christians must be prepared to draw on a wider range of resources, such as social history, sociology, politics, and philosophy, as theology alone is not sufficient to provide convincing analyses of environmental issues. To repeat the words of Genesis or St Francis as if hundreds of years of change in scientific and cultural thought had never happened cannot constitute a reasoned and truthful response to crucial moral and political questions. This does not mean that we have nothing to offer or we cannot become part of the debate, but it does mean that we have a lot of listening and learning to do before we have the right to start making global pronouncements in a relatively new field of human enquiry. One obvious area that Creation Spirituality, for instance, must address, is how, in a political climate that places so much emphasis on individual choice, can environmental concerns become part of a social morality that has real political clout. The history of the most powerful lobby groups, such as the Friends of the Earth, is not exactly encouraging when it comes to genuine political change. This is because environmental, moral issues are not seen as the appropriate concern of government. Market forces are still held up as being the main arbiter of social and political differences. In such a setting, how can environmental pressure groups ever achieve radical change? In which case, Creation Spirituality may appease or entertain the well-meaning Christian conscience, but will have little effect on political policy.

One way of trying to understand what is going on in the environmental movements is to set them within the wider, historical perspective. We tend to see them as a recent phenomenon, forgetting that there is an aspect of their motivation that can be traced back through the last two centuries. Concerns that humanity is despoiling the natural world by its industrial and technological developments go back to the beginnings of the Industrial Revolution. The poetry of William Blake—familiar phrases such as 'dark satanic mills'—and the later writings of John Ruskin and William Morris, each reflect what we might see as a typically British reaction against the darker side of industrial society. The love of nature, the wish to return to a simpler and less destructive way of life and to live in greater harmony is a recurrent theme in our culture. Its influence can be seen in some of the older conservation groups, such as the National Trust and the RSPB. On one level, the more recent environmental pressure groups are carrying on this tradition, although in a more explicitly political manner.

However, such reactions cannot be confined to these islands. There are also strong echoes of German Romanticism, a strand of thought expressed in both literature and philosophy that attempts to redress the imbalance brought about by the Enlightenment. Put simply, it is a rebellion against a society that places all its faith in the powers of human reason. It asks us to look at the consequences of this approach, both in terms of our relationships with the natural world and with each other. It challenges the idea of human progress based on scientific and intellectual development that has gained such a hold in Western culture. There is more to human beings than simply our powers of reason. We are not machines and nature is not simply a resource to be exploited for human profit and benefit. The results of adopting such a myopic approach are potentially catastrophic, as we can now see. While it is vital to have this imbalance redressed, it is important to recognize that the Romantic position swallowed wholesale is equally dangerous. Its emphasis on feelings, intuition and the irrational create a society that is very vulnerable to totalitarian politics. Extreme examples of this are National Socialism in Germany and the Pol Pot regime in Cambodia, both of which contained elements of a 'back to nature' philosophy. The questions that are begged are what is natural and *who* decides what it is and in whose interests? Cut human reason out of it altogether and we are on very dangerous ground.

Essentially, then, contemporary environmental groups, and their religious offshoots, stand within a much broader tradition that is a negative reaction to scientific, technological and mechanistic modes of thought. Also, they can represent a very one-sided interpretation of Western culture, which if translated directly into political action may lead to other dangers. This is not to suggest that they do not represent a necessary corrective to a society that sets too much store in a mechanistic and exploitative approach as there *is* a very real imbalance that needs to be redressed, but whether the Romantics can offer an alternative, viable political and cultural framework for society remains open to question. Perhaps they can best be seen as being part of a system of checks and balances that seeks to limit the worst excesses of industrial society.

One of the limitations of the Romantic view is that it fails to recognize the extent to which our relationship with and understanding of nature are wrapped up in our cultural life. We are no longer faced simply with the alternatives of nature being either wholly distinct from humanity *or* being at one with it, as in the Romantic's vision. As one German writer, Ulrich Beck, has said:

At the end of the twentieth century, nature is neither given nor ascribed, but has, instead, become an historical product, the interior furnishings of the civilizational world, destroyed or endangered in the natural conditions of its reproduction.[3]

In other words, 'nature' is both a social construct (what we imagine it to be or project upon it), and, simultaneously, subject to a whole range of economic and political decisions. It has become absorbed into our cultural life as a source of beauty and peace to be consumed by overstressed workers and, yet, is constantly at risk of destruction because of commercial pressures. Thus:

. . . environmental problems are *not* problems of our surroundings, but are thoroughly social problems, problems of people, their history, their living conditions, their relation to the world and reality, their social, cultural and political situations.[4]

One wonders whether Creation Spirituality has fully grasped this or is, perhaps, still clinging too tightly to the Romantic view.

It is worth noting two points arising from more recent analyses of environmental groups. First, they tend to gain greater support in times of relative affluence. Thus, during the 1970s, they experienced significant growth, but this was slowed down considerably when the economy entered recession. Similarly, there was a resurgence of interest during the mid 1980s, when the benefits of the enterprise culture were at their highest, but the last two or three years of recession have seen people's attention returning to more immediate issues, such as employment and housing. It may be that the issue can only surface effectively when other needs are being securely met.

It is also significant that most of the groups' supporters come from the middle and upper classes. The Green movement, politically and culturally, is not that popular among working-class people, as was the Trade Union movement in its heyday. The relationship between the two is a vexed issue in this country for both the Labour Party and the Liberal Democrats who have sought to woo Green voters. There is a real question as to how deeply environmental concerns have penetrated into the national consciousness. Are most of us fair weather Greens, who revert to capitalistic behaviour when the chips are down, or will the influence of television, schools, and so on have more lasting effects on the younger generation? This remains to be seen.

Second, there is another strand of analysis that suggests that environmental groups are part of a wider movement, which is an attempt to prevent capitalist values encroaching yet further into our normal lives. Thus, our relationship with nature, which has hitherto been a matter of personal and private taste and practice (whether or not we have pets, drive out into the countryside to escape city life, enjoy bird watching, fell walking or whatever) is becoming subject to ever greater statutory interference and, indeed, the profit motive. Paths in the Lake District are being worn away by fell walkers, certain dogs have become a menace, and we have to pay to consume the pleasures of the countryside.

One way of reacting against this is to appeal to older religious ideas, that nature is sacred and, thus, not to be treated in this commercial fashion. Whether this can work in a culture that has largely long since abandoned such views is highly questionable. You cannot re-sanctify nature without believing in a creator God, unless you turn nature itself into some form of deity. Indeed, this is what is happening in some religious strands of the environmental movement. Many Christians will not be happy with this as we are not nature worshippers. Equally, many in our society are unacquainted with God worship and so are even more unlikely to be able to make much sense of the idea of nature being sacred.

What I hope is becoming clear from the analysis so far is that Creation Spirituality needs to be thought of as being part of a wider cultural movement that has its roots in a reaction against both the Enlightenment and Western industrial society. Read a recent document produced by St James's, Piccadilly (the self-styled centre for Creation Spirituality in this country) entitled *1900–2000: A Vision for Ten Years*. In it is a quotation from an American theologian:

> . . . the overriding cultural fact in our generation is the end of the Enlightenment, which is a model of life concerned with control through knowledge, scientific, economic, political, psychological, that is now ending.[5]

I believe such statements are naive and inaccurate. The world described is far from over and, unless we can engage it as it is, it will pass us by as outdated romantics and dreamers. One very clear problem with this view is that the environmental groups themselves are now heavily dependent on scientific findings to support their actions. What we see is not so much the straightforward anti-science and anti-technology approaches of earlier generations, but *science* against science. For instance, theories about the ozone layer require considerable specialized knowledge, not to mention technical facilities and measurement devices not readily available to the lay person.

Perhaps the best description of what is happening is of a growing reflexivity within the scientific world. This is more than simply the routine monitoring of actions and beliefs that humans carry out, but refers to the chronic doubt embedded within science itself, which reminds us that all theories are subject to abandonment or revision in the light of new information or knowledge. Until some scientists established that there were holes in the ozone layer, we were not aware of the dangers of CFCs in aerosols and so on. Almost every day, it seems, a research programme pronounces that a part of our regular diet or a factor in our environment may be bad for our health. The problem for the lay person is knowing how best to assess and react to these statements.

The Enlightenment has certainly *not* ended, in the sense that we have not returned to a pre-scientific view of the world, but, rather, what has occurred is a radicalizing and deepening of those thought processes characteristic of the Enlightenment. Once again, if Creation Spirituality is to have any real relationship with contemporary life, it must face such analyses, not retreat to a romanticized past.

**An analysis of Green and
Creation Spirituality thinking**

I now want to turn to two representative examples of Green or Creation Spirituality. The first, Matthew Fox, would say he stood within the Christian tradition. The second, Charlene Spretnak, is probably Green first, religious second, but I am actually more convinced by her than by Fox. I cannot hope to do justice to Fox's voluminous writings or even to offer a very thorough critique of them here, but will, instead, look at some key themes and reservations.

There is no doubt that Matthew Fox has performed a valuable service for those who wish to relate Christianity to environmental concerns. The work of more mainstream theologians, such as Jürgen Moltmann and Sean McDonagh, has not had the popular impact with both Christians and environmentalists of Fox's *Original Blessing*.[6] The style as well as the content of what he has to say makes him refreshingly readable. I think he has also inadvertently opened up for discussion other questions that regular Christians have felt unable to ask simply by offering a public forum. Unfortunately, I feel that his own input has not been sufficiently worked out to offer a substantial contribution to these wider discussions.

It does show that the churches are missing out by not giving people enough freedom to air their doubts and questions.

This leads to the criteria by which I suggest we should evaluate Creation Spirituality. The main concern that we have expressed is whether such work makes due reference to the level of human operation that is termed critical consciousness. In other words, does it acknowledge the role of our critical and rational faculties in the construction of its theology? In order to decide whether or not this is the case, there are a number of subsidiary questions that can be asked of such material.

First, does it provide the open space within which debates can be freely conducted and genuine disagreements aired? Second, does it take into account the cultural understandings of nature, now determined by social, political and economic decisions, or does it, rather, revert to the Romantic view of a simplistic harmony with nature that denies any role for human reason? Third, does it help us to move towards a moral discourse that will bridge the gap between private and public life so essential if environmental ideas are to have any lasting impact on political policy? Approaches that cannot fulfil these criteria are, indeed, in grave danger of being merely escapist, wishful thinking.

Although Fox has created the opportunity for more open discussion of the issues, and that is probably his greatest contribution, whether or not he then allows for genuine disagreement, I am not so sure. In *Original Blessing*, for instance, he offers a list of 'goodies' and 'baddies' from within the Christian tradition—goodies being those such as Meister Eckhart and Hildegaard of Bingen who have a creation-centred and positive approach towards the natural world in their theology, and baddies including such as St Augustine who have repressed the imaginative and creative aspects of humanity. There is a real danger of caricaturing and scapegoating in this process that does not allow for disagreements. Fox develops his own way of interpreting the Christian tradition that many would want to question.

Fox is certainly very keen on drawing back into the tradition ideas that cohere with the Romantics' harmonious vision of the natural world. The doctrine of original sin is a distortion of Christianity in his view because it creates barriers and destroys harmony. The truth is, he says, that we are in relationship with each other, with the natural world, and with God because that is the original intention of the creation. As others have noted, this seems rather unrealistic. Ideas of sin and brokenness exist not just as some ideological ploy that gives religious institutions power over people—although there is always some truth in that—but because they describe things as we experience them. Harmony is a vision, an ideal, but it is not the reality and we cannot move towards that vision simply by denying the reality, which is what Fox appears to do. We have to deal with things as they are, broken, messy, ambiguous, compromised, and, often, painful. A faith that speaks to these conditions seems to me more appropriate, more realistic.

My major problem with Fox is that I do not believe that he provides us with an effective way in to the political dimension of the environmental question. Political life is undeniably messy, but it is where most of the power lies and most of the crucial decisions are made, so Fox's work, while attractive and stimulating to read, will not have much impact at that level. It appeals to some questioning Christians and some on the fringes of established religion. He does draw on non-Christian sources and some would see him verging on paganism or some form of nature worship. The dangers here are not so much of unorthodoxy, but of a naive return to nature that unleashes irrational forces, themselves damaging to humanity. Like the Romantics, he is correct to say that there is more to human beings than just reason, but wrong to reduce us to bundles of pure feelings, intuition and imagination alone. I would want to say that the creativity he so values *must* involve both aspects of human nature.

Now to my second example, Charlene Spretnak. Her book,

A Critique of Creation Spirituality

The Spiritual Dimension of Green Politics[7], is well worth reading. Unlike Fox, she makes it quite explicit that ecology comes first and Christianity second. She believes that the well-being and fruitfulness of human and non-human life on earth have inherent value and that the richness and diversity of lifeforms contributes to the realization of these values. Therefore, human beings have no right to reduce this richness and diversity except to satisfy vital needs. This, presumably, could entail a no-growth economy, not an obviously popular political programme. She wants to see the decentralization of political and economic power and the development of both on a sustainable and appropriate scale. Visionary stuff no doubt, but at least she does attempt to tackle the political dimensions of such issues.

On the question of human reason, she is much more balanced, in my opinion, than Fox. For her, ecological thinking is not a retreat from reason, but an enlargement of it to a more comprehensive and, thus, efficient means of analysis. We need the maturity to value both freedom and tradition, the individual and the community, science and nature, male and female. It is no good trying to make the Enlightenment the scapegoat of the environmental crisis. These are words of wisdom with which I think many Christians could concur. She believes in creating the spaces for people to do their own thinking on issues rather than being presented with pre-packaged answers. Religious, social and political life should reflect the ecological insights of interdependence, respecting differences while searching for common ground. Spirituality enables us to grasp and move towards that vision of inter-connectedness in which we experience relationships as they could be at their best. This is very close to Fox, but she does not seem to confuse the vision with the reality.

The main problem I have with Spretnak is that she hangs on to the idea of re-sanctifying nature, which, I believe, creates too many problems. I think it also conflicts with her own view that the spirituality we now require is not a denial of reason, but a further development of it. I do not believe that a post-Enlightenment, post-modern culture, which is what she is advocating, can make a return to religious ideas that represent an irrational or pre-rational response. If these ideas did catch hold, as some within Creation Spirituality would wish them to do, they would only ever appeal to a small and isolated minority of people who would not have the political insight or influence to implement the other programmes she proposes. If we are in a 'pick and mix' religious market-place now, many of us will have good reasons not to select a pre-Enlightenment view of nature. We are more likely to look for an approach that goes beyond the mechanistic, but, perhaps, draws on quantum physics as a more appropriate resource for and picture of reality. However, with this one major reservation, I do feel that Spretnak offers us some vital clues in finding a viable way forward.

Conclusion

We have seen now both some of the limitations and promise of Creation or Green Spirituality. I have not been able to review in detail all the contributors to this field, but I hope that the basic arguments of this area of thought are clear. The question remains, what sort of spirituality might constitute an appropriate Christian response to the environmental debate? I phrase it that way because my instinct is that the writers we have looked at are correct in searching for a spirituality rather than a theology in the traditional sense. Attempts to rework and reinterpret Christian doctrine are of interest only to a few, even within the church. Most people require a more practical and immediate response, and those on the fringes of, or beyond, Christianity seem more likely to find common ground in the broad area of spirituality.

I think that what we are still missing are two vital and related elements. First, we require a fuller, more inclusive model of what it is to be a human being, such as that proposed in the third mediating framework. The problem with some of the proponents of this new approach is that they deny or reduce the role of human reason. They wish to jump from the level of intuition and feeling to that of a transrational consciousness, within which the boundaries between ourselves and the rest of creation become blurred or disappear and we merge into oneness, or whatever. Some ecologists have talked of the 'ecological self' with this in mind. It is these altered states of consciousness that link very powerfully with strands of Christian mystical thought (see, for instance, Meister Eckhart and Martin Israel).

This is acceptable to the extent that most of us do, at some time, experience being at one with the natural world, and this is to be valued. I am not happy, though, when these experiences become a form of escapism from reality and detract from practical action. If we retain a role for human reason within our model of humanity, then we can come back down to earth and translate some of the vision into our everyday lives.

Similarly, we must beware of bypassing or denigrating science, technology or politics, or of making the Enlightenment the scapegoat for our environmental problems. These are vital and valuable spheres of human activity that are, indeed, open to distortion and abuse, but the way to deal with these abuses is not to abandon the whole field, but to go on working faithfully within it, being aware of the dangers and ambiguities. A spirituality that ignores these dimensions consigns itself to a Romantic ghetto. Strangely enough, withdrawal from the world can only be justified if it leads back to and enhances a more radical engagement with the world.

We have, then, established a critique of Creation Spirituality. We need to decide whether it is merely Romantic escapism, or a vision for the future. The answer is that it can be both. It is Romantic escapism when it denies a role for human reason and offers no grounds for realistic political involvement, but it is a vision for the future when it gives us glimpses of the restoration of relationships with creation, which is the great hope of the Christian tradition.

Notes

1 Anna Bramwell, *Ecology in the Twentieth Century: A History*. New Haven, CT, Yale University Press, 1989.
2 Matthew Fox in Philip N. Joranson and Ken Butigan, eds, *Cry of the Environment* (Santa Fe, Bear and Co., 1984), p. 87.
3 Ulrich Beck, *Risk Society* (Sage 1992), p. 80.
4 Beck, p. 81.
5 The quotation is from the American Old Testament scholar Walter Brueggemann.
6 For instance: Jürgen Moltmann, *God in Creation* (SCM Press 1985); Sean McDonagh, *To Care for the Earth* (Geoffrey Chapman 1986), and Matthew Fox, *Original Blessing* (Santa Fe, Bear and Co., 1983).
7 Charlene Spretnak, *The Spiritual Dimension of Green Politics*. Santa Fe, Bear and Co., 1986.

7

Local Theology
and the Church

Poppy seed head theology

At the beginning of the book the task that was set was that of
establishing a way of doing theology that could make the
connections between everyday experience and the insights of
the Christian tradition. The process of local theology has been
offered as one way in which that tradition can be brought to
life. This was visualized as poppy seeds being blown out in
different directions and leading to growth in sometimes
unexpected places. We have seen how a local group can,
together, identify problems and issues, and then release its
members to initiate appropriate responses. These, in turn,
stimulate questions that are of more than local significance
and require the analytical resources of disciplines such as
sociology and psychology. Through the three mediating
frameworks it has been possible to move beyond the local
and engage in wider discussion. However, this cannot be the
end of the story.

It has become clear that this approach to theology is somewhat radical in nature. Instead of starting with doctrinal
statements that then have to be applied to contemporary life,
it begins with local activity and encourages a process of
reflection, drawing on whatever sources seem appropriate. It
is not even assumed in advance that ideas or symbols from
the Christian faith community are going to be of help in this
process. There is, thus, a freedom and a scope for interpretation

that some Christians may see as threatening. However, if we are to engage with other groups that form the context in which we are now working, I suggest that such risks are inescapable if we are to get anywhere.

Poppy seed head theology stands broadly within an approach that I will describe as the religion of resistance. To adopt a sociological perspective for a moment, it seems that religion can perform one of three functions within a society: it can be legitimating, integrating, or critical. In other words, it can be used to support the status quo, it can provide a sense of belonging and identity, or it can be employed as a motivating factor in struggling towards new and more just forms of social life. It is the third of these that can also be termed the religion of resistance. In each of our local projects, there was an underlying concern to work for improvements in relationships between groups, both inside and outside the church, and, indeed, in the relationship between humanity and the natural world. For the Christians involved, this reflected beliefs about the nature of God and humanity's role within creation.

Local theology, with its basis in practical engagement and its willingness to use wider resources, is well equipped for a stance of resistance and protest. It resists the temptation to impose external interpretations and make universal claims for the approaches it adopts. Above all, it aims to help people discover resonances from within the stories and symbols of the faith community that then illuminate both the Christian tradition and the contemporary situation. This cannot happen without a desire and confidence to participate in the critical reflection that we have described as essential for level three— the critical consciousness. A faith that either bypasses this or denies its importance cannot retain much credibility. However, equally, a faith that does not then go beyond this to search for a still centre in the midst of this flux, created by provisionality and contingency, will cease to hold people's trust and faith.

The elements of modernity

The method developed so far has emerged as a response to a *local* situation. This now needs to be tested to see whether or not it is an appropriate response to the wider social and intellectual environment. If theology is to be truly contextual as well as local, then it needs to establish its validity at both levels.

In order to map out the territory, I will use an analytical framework proposed by Giddens as a starting point, but make some significant alterations.[1]

The first characteristic of the modern era is the abandonment of what post-structuralist philosophers have termed 'the grand narratives'. As you will recall, these are explanations or ways of looking at the world that have claimed to offer definitive understandings of the world and humanity's place within it, including religious belief systems, but also all scientific theories. Each of these can only have a relative value, in that no single theory can claim to give the whole picture. The other key argument is that we are now aware that there are different ways of looking at the world, not just that of the tradition in which we might have been brought up. How are we to know which of these is the right one?

The Enlightenment's answer was that human reason was capable of carrying out this task, but we can now see that this, too, is just another grand narrative that has lent itself to ideological distortion by claiming to have universal validity. If this is the end of the story, then all we have are a host of different pictures or world views, including Christianity, and no way of judging between them; there is no privileged position from which we can establish an evaluation of these varied frameworks.

This is the main reason narrative has been accorded greater importance in moral philosophy. The only position from which one can make moral judgements is from inside one of these traditions or the narrative in which it is enshrined. The danger of this is that it is difficult to see how people from different traditions can conduct a reasoned discussion when there is no common ground between them. If not even the powers of reason are common to all human beings, then we seem to retreat to a form of intellectual tribalism.

Telling the local stories in local theology is a way of acknowledging these problems and of avoiding the imposition of centralized theological interpretation normally offered by the wider church. It helps to reconstruct an experiential and contextualized basis for the theological response. However, if this were all there was, we would soon have as many different theologies as groups adopting a local approach and they, too, might experience difficulty in communicating with other groups of Christians. There does need to be further common ground, some shared framework within which we can conduct all our discussions and handle all our conflicts.

Even this, though, will not be adequate when it comes to communicating with non-Christians, which, as we have seen, is another vital aspect of local theology. There must be other common ground if we are not to remain trapped within the confines of our own tradition. In this sense, the original Enlightenment project is still alive, even though it cannot claim to offer a definitive answer to this question. In any case, experience shows that we do communicate effectively with those who do not share our beliefs, so how is this possible? The mediating frameworks I have proposed are, I hope, examples of the way in which this communication can occur.

What this rather complicated philosophical discussion shows is that the contemporary context requires a theology that can take local narratives as its starting point, but that the process of reflection needs to carry people beyond this in order to communicate with other Christians and those from other traditions.

The second characteristic of modernity, according to Giddens, is the central role played by the polarity of risk and trust. We are now increasingly aware of the threats of nuclear war and environmental disaster that could destroy not just individual lives but humanity's very existence on this planet. The way that we cope with this most of the time is to push it to the back of our minds, but this is only possible if we have already received an early life dosage of trust that enables us to believe that all will be well. This is not simply escapism, but a crucial human means of dealing with what Giddens calls 'ontological insecurity'.

Our awareness of the risks requires us to possess this antidote of trust. Without it we would fall into despair. The particular forms that this takes in modern society are, first, a trust in expert systems, such as modes of transport and communication, and, second, a confidence in the reliability of other people, including those outside our immediate circle of family and friends. We mentioned this in the context of the new forms of trust that are necessary for community life.

This links back to local theology in two ways. It is clear that all of us need some form of support from others in our lives, particularly at times of stress or tragedy. It is legitimate that Christianity should provide love and metaphorical hugs when these are needed. Once again, this can be an appropriate starting point for theological reflection, on its own, it can lead to a narrow and underdeveloped understanding of Christianity. Christianity cannot, ultimately, provide a safe haven from the world, nor should it seek to do so. Instead, it should aim to encourage the growth that comes from greater self-confidence and trust.

This is what we learned from the local community projects. It can be enabled via the experience of participating in schemes that rely on people taking local initiatives and following them through. It still helps to have somebody else to hold our hands in the early stages, but greater confidence, and, indeed, hope, emerge as the projects begin to gather momentum. So, we can say that involvement in this type of scheme is an appropriate way of building up the greater levels of trust necessary for a renewed community life and combatting ontological insecurity.

The third characteristic of modern life relevant to a local theology is what Giddens calls 'reflexivity'. What he means by this is the growing tendency to reflect critically on all aspects of our lives. This is particularly significant for our attitude towards tradition. Very little is now taken for granted, and many of us are constantly engaged in the process of reviewing how we behave and what we believe to see if all is acceptable and appropriate. This is probably a result of our awareness of other traditions and ways of going about things. There are always other possibilities, so why did I choose this one, and is it the right one? This self-monitoring itself becomes a factor in future patterns of relationship.

This approach is reflected in local theology's critical appropriation of the Christian tradition. In particular, it will search out and enter into the critique process in instances where Christianity is being used to legitimize unjust power structures. However, this will also involve the critical inter-pretation of insights from elsewhere, for instance sociology or psychology. Each of these potential contributions has to be thought through in the light of wider considerations, such as alternative viewpoints from within the discipline.

So far, we have been able to use Giddens' framework without critical comment, but his interpretation of religion needs now to be brought into question. It becomes clear from what he says about environments of risk and trust that he views religion as essentially bound to tradition in a way that prevents it being future-oriented. So, for instance, when he suggests what the key categories of trust were in pre-modern society, he lists religious cosmologies along with tradition, the local community, and kinship relations. These provided the overall context in which people of that period could build up their trust. In modern society, how-ever, the key categories are personal friendships, often involving sexual intimacy, expert systems, and a confidence in the future. I would want to challenge the implication that religion cannot be future-orientated.

Local Theology and the Church

Local theology, as with many contextual theologies, is an attempt to develop an approach that looks forward. There is nothing particularly radical about this as Christianity has the symbol of the kingdom of God to keep our eyes firmly fixed on the future. It is true that the church can and has used Christian teaching as a conservative force, but there are also critical and prophetic elements in the faith that would bring this into question. Giddens' failure to recognize this potential in the Christian position leads him to ignore the role that a radical theology might play in an overall response to modernity.

This is unfortunate, but it represents a not uncommon failing among sociologists to confine the relevance of religion to the past. Such a view tends to result from a concentration on dogma rather than on observation. The question that should be asked is, given that religion can and does still play a role in people's lives, what sort of contribution can it make to the common human struggle for a better future? If Giddens had asked himself this, he would have been able to make the connection between new forms of theology and his closing comments on responses to modernity.

He makes much of the notion of trust, as we have seen, but descibes it as a project that now has to be worked out by groups and individuals. I would want to agree with this on the basis of local experience. However, his dismissal of religion leads him to neglect one vital question. Why should anybody want to bother with such a project when the chances of success seem so slim? Giddens might want to claim that the search for new forms of intimacy and trust are a psychological necessity in the face of ontological insecurity, but I am not convinced that this could ever be established. It is the case that people are engaged in this project, but what is their real motivation and what sustains them in the task?

Within a Christian context, I would want to return to the idea of a commitment to the other as a key motivating and sustaining factor. The demands and dangers of establishing the sort of relationships being suggested are such that many would shy away from them unless they saw this as an expression of this very commitment. Perhaps loving God by loving one's neighbour now requires this form of relationship. Bonds of mutual respect and concern previously linking people within close-knit communities did not require this type of personal knowledge of the other. Now, though, we have to be able to establish such bonds with complete strangers day by day, and the necessary trust involved in doing so can only be based on a supposed greater knowledge of both oneself and others.

This, perhaps, helps to explain the growth in counselling and therapy. How can I be the person that I need to be in these close relationships with others if I cannot understand who and what I am? The current concern with self-awareness is also part of the reflexivity described by Giddens. It is also a major factor in many of the new social movements and the search for identity to which they give expression. There is a very real danger that this will be reduced to the individual level and thus ignore the equally vital question of social and political relationships. A local theology, itself enshrining a commitment to the other can fruitfully bring these concerns to the surface and hold on to the importance of linking private and public life. It can also motivate the search for new forms of intimacy and trust.

Finally, this commitment has an important contribution to make to the discussion at the beginning of this chapter of the need for a revised understanding of human reason. The Enlightenment tradition has lost its credibility largely because reason has been turned into a tool for achieving specific aims in modern industrial society. In other words, the human capacity to think things through and argue them out is valued mainly because it has led to more efficient, productive, profitable, commercial, and industrial systems. It often appears as though the real aim of education is to prepare young people to be effective and reliable cogs in the capitalist machine rather than to encourage them to think for themselves and make reasoned moral judgements. Thus, the original Enlightenment hope, that releasing the power of reason from the bondage of tradition would lead to a better world and greater human maturity, has been dashed. What we have instead is described as instrumental reason, which serves only the purposes of those with power and treats human beings as means to an end.

The alternative understanding of reason outlined earlier in this chapter is, in one way, a revival of the original Enlightenment hope. Perhaps in the structures of communication there is a framework that will support and encourage thought and argument that will not just fall prey to the pressures of industrial society. The problem with this is to prevent it becoming another grand narrative, which can be used as an instrument of repression. If this could happen, language would have to be used to offer others the chance to be and become themselves, and to show that they are valued in their own right.

If there is a prior commitment to the other person, then it can be argued that communication should work in this way, and instances where it is not can be identified and criticized. The aim is open communication in which all, by virtue of being human, are offered the opportunity to participate. The Local History Group and the community projects certainly had this aim. Much of the criticism of local power structures revolved around their unwillingness to allow certain groups a voice in decisions about their future. Even the act of gathering local stories had as one of its objectives to affirm and value those who were rarely listened to. It would seem that this communicative reason does operate in some circumstances.

New social movements

I hope it is clear by now that the internal dynamic of the process I have been describing as local theology is local engagement that implicates wider questioning and debates;

the poppy seed head explodes, scattering seeds in different directions. Thus, as we have seen, some of the theory behind local theology is consistent with an analysis of the wider cultural context, but what about the practice? Is there any evidence that the ways of working developed in South West Shropshire are of wider relevance and application? If not, then what we have witnessed might just be a one off, possible in only very limited circumstances. I want to suggest that an examination of what are called new social movements will show that this is not the case, but that there are parallels with other groups that need to be taken into account as we consider the implications of local theology for the wider church. In particular, there is much common ground with the religion of resistance, of which local theology is characteristic.

What do we mean by new social movements? The most obvious examples are the environmental and the women's movements. The civil rights groups in the United States would also fit into this category. There is nothing magic about the term, it is simply a general way of describing the ways in which human beings have acted in consort to bring about social change. Trade unions could be classed as social movements because they represent bands of workers, organized on a collective basis, to fight for basic rights for employees and to gain better working conditions for them.

We need to be aware that there are debates surrounding this term within sociology. First, in what respects are current social movements different from the early trade unions, for instance? In other words, what justifies the use of the word 'new'? Second, is there a danger of over-generalizing and, thus, giving the impression of a homogeneous set of groups when the reality is more complicated and varied? Third, there is disagreement over how such movements should be studied. Should energy be concentrated on discovering *how* they operate and come into being, or should it be given to trying to answer the question as to *why* they have come into being in the first place?[2]

This is a large and varied area of debate, but suffice to say that I am going to assume here that there is a valid sense in which we can talk about *new* social movements as differing from previous social movements in important ways as they relate to the political and economic environment in which they have arisen. It is also important to acknowledge the danger of over-generalization and be aware that there are differences between movements and, indeed, within movements themselves. There is for instance wide variety in the ways that environmental groups operate. Finally, it is important to be able to utilize the insights of different approaches to the study of new social movements and answer the questions of how *and* why they have come into being.

We need to recognize that many new social movements are addressing the same issues as more radical Christian groups—the problems of racism, social attitudes towards women, the environment and so on. On this level, often a cause will be common to both groups, and, indeed, there may be an overlap in personnel, too. Beneath this often lies a much deeper concern about questions of meaning and purpose, and a feeling that there is more to life than being a passive consumer in a restrictive capitalist system. There is certainly an argument that new social movements are trying to articulate what would traditionally be considered religious questions, but, because of the way in which institutionalized religion is so often bound up with existing power structures, these questions have to find another focus. The church is also so concerned with its own survival that it fails to do justice to the more fundamental human questions that their faith raises and tries to answer.

One can interpret these questions within a framework of the basic set of relationships that constitute human life. Thus, there is the relationship between the individual and the state. This is questioned in the movements for democratic reform in Eastern Europe and in the demands for greater participatory democracy in certain sections of the Green movement. There is the relationship of the individual to their self, which is reflected in the search for new personal identity through psychotherapy and new sexual freedom. Both young people and those experiencing so-called mid-life crises are questioning the models of human nature being imposed by a capitalist culture, and there is talk, too, of the ecological self, which acknowledges a sense of unity with nature. The environmental movement can be seen to be providing a focus for these questions.

The relationship between male and female is another key area of current debate and here it is the women's movement that is striving towards new definitions and understandings. Then, of course, there is humanity's relationship to the natural world, as represented by the environmental movement once again. The only question of relationship *not* explicitly tackled by new social movements is probably that of humanity's relationship to God, but this begs so much that it remains largely implicit, although the term 'spirituality' is used by a number of people within new social movements, and this suggests a search for a dimension to life that is being ignored or suppressed in contemporary society.

It would be a mistake to overemphasize these themes as this could then sound like a belated Christian attempt to appropriate and domesticate new social movements. However, there is a case to be made that the latter are raising questions for which Christianity has claimed to have answers. Perhaps the problem is that the answers no longer convince because they appear to have become divorced from experience, in which case, one must begin all over again by just asking the questions. The church might do well to swallow some of its pride and go back to the same starting point without assuming that it has anything to offer. Local theology is an attempt to do just that.

If there is much potential overlap in terms of content between new social movements and a radical theology, then there is even more so in terms of methods of operation. The most obvious example of this is the use of networking—a way of overcoming geographical and time boundaries by using modern technology such as the telephone and fax machine. Many new social movements are deliberately loose in their organization, perhaps having no official membership or records. This both makes them harder to pin down and keep under surveillance, and prevents power structures building up within the group. It is interesting that the Local History Group operated in this way and it is not the *modus operandi* of most church groups, but it worked.

Approaches to power are another key point of common concern. New social movements work to make power visible, to bring it to the surface where it can be seen and then challenged. Thus, the need for demonstrations and the use of the media and the dangers of being labelled as troublemakers. Offe's analysis applies here, as it did in our local attempt to challenge the power within the Parish Council. It is also important that the way in which the movements work does not contradict the messages about power that they are trying to convey. In a sense, the medium becomes the message, even if this means losing out to the more traditional methods of exercising power. It is better to lose the battle than resort to the opposition's tactics.

Summing up, we can say that new social movements can be seen to possess four novel structural characteristics. First, they are concerned with signs and symbols, with what people believe and how these beliefs are expressed in practical action, particularly through relationships—they are not interested in gaining economic or social advantages for their members. Second, they emphasize the importance of the way things are done and participation as the means of learning new ways and of challenging the old. Third, they are an attempt to cross the boundary between private and public life, now so firmly set in contemporary society, and to highlight the value of collective action in an age that appears to worship the individual. Finally, they reflect an awareness of the global dimension of the problems now facing humanity and the need for a new approach that does not just reduce all relationships to their instrumental value.

All of this suggests that there is much common ground between new social movements and the developing radical theologies, the religion of resistance. What are the implications of this for the church? First, there must, surely, be a greater willingness among Christians to acknowledge that others are asking the sort of questions normally associated with religious beliefs. This must not mean that Christians then leap in with their stock answers, but, instead, be prepared to engage at the beginning of the questioning process. This entails tempering the claims that can be made for Christianity itself. We do *not* have all the answers; we may not even be asking all the right questions. So often, it is social movements that force issues on to the church's agenda.

Second, there should be a willingness to experiment with new forms of congregational life. The old institutional models are inhibiting new life and are so wrapped up in the struggle for survival that they direct what energy remains into unfruitful channels. Networking is one possible way forward, and some Christian groups have already started to operate this system. The days of Christians gathering together solely on the basis of geographical locality are surely numbered. The changing patterns of social life that have so clearly emerged in our local study may force the churches to recognize that parish boundaries are of decreasing relevance to most people. Even in Shropshire, kinship ties were more important to local people than parochial loyalties.

Third, Christians must look again at the question of power, as we began to do in an earlier chapter. So much of what we claim to stand for is distorted in practice because of the power structures within which we operate. There is no point preaching about empowerment, or, indeed, justice, unless we can exercise both within our own organizational and congregational life. This may mean letting go of theology, among other things, for this has so often been a way of sustaining control over the beliefs and behaviour of others. A local theology can give people greater freedom to think issues through for themselves without having interpretations and ideas imposed on them by the central church. There also needs to be a critique of forms of theology that collude with existing power structures and merely legitimate a success ethic or an enterprise culture.

Fourth, Christians need to acknowledge the global scale of the problems that we now face and the urgency of working towards an ethical stance that can draw together different faiths and cultures so that a common response becomes possible. This, again, entails a willingness to bracket some of the claims that Christianity has been accustomed to make for itself, taking its place alongside other faiths and traditions struggling towards an appropriate future rather than assuming it is the only way. This is, indeed, a challenge to orthodoxy, but then orthodoxy has not had to face this situation before. We must not make the reductionist mistake of assuming that acknowledging the relative value of our tradition implies abandoning insight and conviction.

This is quite a programme and leads to the final question: how optimistic should we be about the capacity of new social movements and the religion of resistance to bring about the necessary changes? Identifying a way forward is not the same as assuming that it will be possible to implement it, nor does it encourage the kind of arrogance that pronounces that this heralds the kingdom, or however we might wish to describe that which we are working towards. It is only a *possible* way forward, for which we can present warrants and justifications. What we must not forget are, first, the unintended consequences of human action—the results we cannot foresee that constantly foil the best-laid plans—and, second, the influence of the economic and political environment in which this is taking place.

To concentrate for a moment on the second of those, there is a serious question as to whether new social movements are simply defensive movements trying to hold back the boundaries of social life against the increasingly pervasive influence of government and commerce, or whether they possess real emancipatory potential. The dilemma is that faced by all protest movements in any age: how do you get close enough to the centres of power in order to bring about change without being swallowed up by the very system you are opposing? For instance, some aspects of the Green movement are now being turned to financial advantage by commercial interests. Is this changing the system or merely colluding with it? The same ambiguity is present in community work (as we realized in our own local projects) in that, within a political environment that has a vested interest in advocating self-help, it can be used as an excuse for withdrawing central resources. All of these projects are riddled with ambiguity because they can be exploited by those already in power.

There is a further complication. Both community and environmental movements, for instance, could be interpreted as attempts to keep things as they are, rather than as genuine moves forward. Let us keep our balanced community or our traditional hay meadow. If this is all there is to it, then this is no more than a form of escapism. Here, again, we have to acknowledge an ambiguity. The movements *can* be used in such a way, as can Christianity, merely as a safe haven. Is it resistance to change *per se*, or to some specific changes that are seen to be damaging to ourselves and others?

The movements need to be placed on the axis of power suggested in Chapter 2, only then can we begin to see whether or not they represent emancipatory potential. Having said this, I still believe that the local experience suggests that new social movements are a better bet for a positive way forward than any other political movement, and that the religion of resistance, likewise, holds more hope for the future. The only way to test this out is to try it and see, and it is this opportunity that a local theology can offer the church. Learning to work together with the aim of resisting instances of the unjust and unjustified uses of power is the most practical way of keeping alive the alternatives that are embodied in the symbols of the faith community.

Notes

1 Anthony Giddens, *The Consequences of Modernity*. Polity Press 1990. See also Giddens, *Modernity and Self-Identity* (Polity Press 1991) and *The Transformation of Intimacy* (Polity Press 1992).

2 See Ron Eyerman and Andrew Jamison, *Social Movements: A Cognitive Approach*. Polity Press 1991.

Index

Index